Clearly Math
Grade 1

Written by Robyn Silbey

Illustrated by Mark Mason

Editor: Stephanie Garcia
Copy Editors: Michael Batty, Robert Newman
Book Design: Anthony D. Paular
Graphic Artist: Daniel Willits
J331001 Clearly Math Grade 1

All rights reserved—Printed in the U.S.A.
Copyright © 2001 Judy/Instructo
A Division of Frank Schaffer Publications, Inc.
23740 Hawthorne Blvd., Torrance, CA 90505

Notice! Pages may be reproduced for classroom or home use only, not for commercial resale. No part of this publication may be reproduced for storage in a retrieval system or transmitted in any form or by any means—electronic, mechanical, recording, etc.—without the prior written permission of the publisher. Reproduction of these materials for an entire school or school system is strictly prohibited.

Table of Contents

Introduction 3

Number Sense
  Extension activity pages 4
  Spin and Draw (Numbers 1 to 10) 7
  Match Game (Reading and Writing
    Two-Digit Numbers) 8
  A Greater Gator (Comparing Numbers) ... 9
  Follow the Dots (Order; Skip Counting
    by Fives) 10
  Up, Down, All Around (Number Patterns
    on a Hundred Chart) 11

Addition
  Extension activity pages 12
  Colorful Sums (Sums up to 10) 14
  Secret Message (Making a Ten) 15
  Drawing Doubles (Using Doubles to Add) ... 16
  Mix 'n' Match (Practice Facts to 18) 17
  Shop for Stickers (Problem Solving
    with Addition) 18
  B-I-N-G-O (Adding One- and
    Two-Digit numbers) 19

Subtraction
  Extension activity pages 20
  Color the Differences (Differences from
    10 or Less) 23
  Magic Subtraction Squares (Differences
    from 18 or Less) 24
  In the Bag (Missing Addends) 25
  Compare Costs (Problem Solving
    with Subtraction) 26
  Dot's My Family! (Fact Families) 27
  Follow the Path (Choose the Operation) ... 28
  A Cross-Number Puzzle (Subtracting
    One-Digit from Two-Digit Numbers) ... 29

Geometry and Fractions
  Extension activity pages 30
  Cross Out (Attributes of Solid Shapes) ... 32
  Color by Shape (Attributes of
    Plane Shapes) 33
  Matching Halves (Symmetry) 34
  Fraction Path (Identifying Halves, Thirds,
    and Fourths) 35

Time, Measurement, and Money
  Extension activity pages 36
  Hour Match Game (Time to the Hour) ... 39
  The Wrong Time (Telling Time to
    the Half Hour) 40
  The Hands of Time (Showing Time
    on a Clock) 41
  Inch by Inch (Measuring in Inches) 42
  Shopping for Stickers (Choosing Coins
    to Pay for Items) 43
  Mystery Purse (Counting Coin Collections) ... 44
  Pocket Change (Using Different Coins to
    Show the Same Amount) 45

Data and Probability
  Extension activity pages 46
  Playtime Table (Making Tally Tables) 48
  Picture This! (Reading a Pictograph) 49
  Pattern Block Graph (Making a
    Bar Graph) 50
  Pattern Power (Identifying and
    Continuing Patterns) 51

Teacher Aid: Dot Paper 52

Teacher Aid: Pattern Blocks 53

Answers 54

Transparencies
  T1: *Hundred Chart* 57
  T2: *Number Lines* 58
  T3: *Ten-Frames and Two-Color Counters* ... 59
  T4: *Sticker Store* 60
  T5: *Pattern Block Design* 61
  T6: *Judy Clock* 62
  T7: *Rulers and Coins* 63
  T8: *Graphing Grid* 64

Introduction

Clearly Math is designed to help students develop a deep understanding of basic math concepts taught in first grade. Focus areas of study complement the NCTM Principles and Standards for School Mathematics (PSSM). *Clearly Math* encourages students to think creatively and critically. Questions are provided, both in activities and on the reproducibles, that can be used as springboards for rich classroom discussions. The activities in *Clearly Math* help students apply their skills and knowledge in a variety of formats and presentations.

Clearly Math content areas of study are separated into six strands. Each strand features hands-on, minds-on concept-building activities as well as several reproducibles. As an added bonus, *Clearly Math* features a collection of *full-color transparencies* for use throughout the book. A special box near the title of the activity or on the reproducible page tells you that a transparency is recommended for best results. Place the transparency on an overhead projector and present the activity or reproducible to your students. You are all set for a successful lesson that requires little preparation time for you.

Finally, *Clearly Math* contains assessment activities that evaluate conceptual understanding. These activities, labeled Assessing Conceptual Understanding (ACU), appear in each unit and can be evaluated using the rubric below.

Clearly Math can be used all year to captivate students and enrich math instruction.

Tips for Using the Transparency Pages

These transparency pages include interdisciplinary connections and teaching aids. Here are some tips on how to use and store them:

1. The transparencies may be duplicated for use by individual students or groups of students when completing some of the activities in this book. The full-color feature of the transparencies will add interest to the activities when used on an overhead projector. The colors will become gray when photocopied, but the pages will still be usable by the students.

2. Some of the transparencies are meant to be cut apart and used as manipulatives on the overhead projector. It is recommended that you make photocopies before cutting transparencies apart, to be kept with the pieces.

3. You may wish to store some of your transparencies in envelopes. Add holes to the envelopes with a three-hole punch, put the pieces in the envelopes, and put the envelopes in a binder. Be sure to label each envelope.

Rubric for Assessing Conceptual Understanding ACU Activities

3 The child's performance or work sample shows a thorough understanding of the topic. Work is clearly explained with examples and/or words, all calculations are correct, and explanations reflect reasoning beyond the simplicity of the calculations.

2 The child's performance or work sample shows a good understanding of the topic. There may be some errors in calculations, but the work reflects a general knowledge of details and a reasonable understanding of mathematical ideas.

1 The child's performance or work sample shows a limited understanding of the topic. The written work does not reflect understanding of the problem, and examples contain errors.

0 The child's performance or work sample is too weak to evaluate or is nonexistent.

Number Sense

Play Go Fish

Children will learn all about numbers simply by making the cards for this popular game. And once the cards are made, they'll want to play again and again!

1. Have the children work in groups of four. Provide each group with forty 5" x 7" index cards.
2. Have the children make cards that describe each number from 1 to 10 as follows:

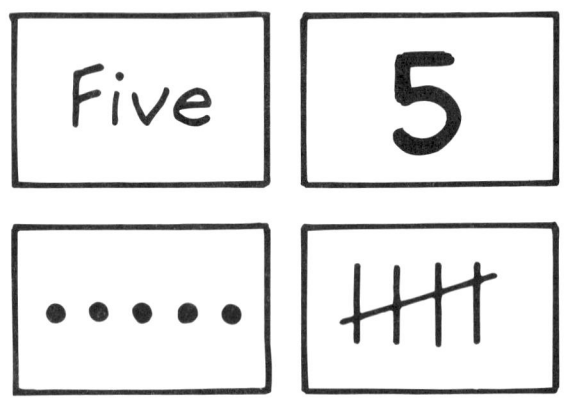

3. When all of the cards have been made, each group of four children should mix and place the cards facedown on the table between them.
4. Each child per group draws five cards for his or her hand.
5. Have the children play Go Fish, asking each other for cards that will make a "book" of any given number.
6. Play continues until all books are made.

Tic-Tac-Toe

This game provides a fun way for children to learn how to recognize numbers from 1 to 9, from 10 to 19, decade numbers, or any other group of numbers.

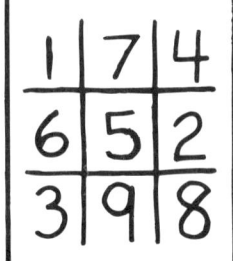

1. Provide pairs of children with plain paper and nine counters. Each pair draws a tic-tac-toe board on a plain sheet of paper.
2. Have children in each pair write numbers 1–9 in any order in the boxes formed by the board.
3. Call out a number and have one child in each pair place a counter red-side up over that number on the tic-tac-toe board.
4. Call out a second number. The child's partner places a counter yellow-side up over that number on the board.
5. Continue until one child gets tic-tac-toe or all numbers are called. Repeat as time and interest permit.

Guess My Pattern

Transparency 1

1. Reproduce the *Hundred Chart* transparency and distribute one copy per pair of children. Supply each pair with several beans or small counters.
2. Write a pattern with one missing number on the chalkboard. Have children place beans on the hundred chart to mark the pattern.

   10, 20, 30, 40, 50, ___ (60)
   1, 3, 5, 7, ___, 11, 13 (9)

3. Invite children in each pair to discuss the pattern with their partners and suggest possibilities for the missing number in the pattern.
4. Encourage the children to make up their own patterns. After you have approved the patterns, have children challenge classmates to guess their patterns.

© Judy/Instructo J331001 Clearly Math • Grade 1

Skip-Counting Patterns

Transparency 1

Use the *Hundred Chart* transparency to help children recognize number patterns and skip-count by intervals of 2, 5, and 10.

1. To count by tens, have children identify the number 10 and its multiples on the hundred chart. Encourage children to recognize the pattern that the numbers form on the chart (a straight line from top to bottom in the far-right column). Children should notice that the numbers are all the same color.

2. Invite a volunteer to come to the overhead projector and point to each number as his or her classmates say it aloud.

3. To count by fives, have children identify the number 5 on the hundred chart. Circle it. Guide them five squares up to find the next number in the sequence (10) and circle it on the chart. Repeat several times until children are able to describe the pattern on the chart (the numbers form two straight lines from top to bottom in the middle and right columns).

4. When all multiples of five are circled, invite a volunteer to come to the overhead projector and point to each number as his or her classmates say it aloud.

5. To count by twos, have children identify the number 2 on the hundred chart. Repeat the procedure outlined in Step 3 in intervals of two. Children should see that skip-counting by twos results in patterns of alternating marked and unmarked vertical rows on the hundred chart.

1	2	3	4	(5)	6	7	8	9	10
11	12	13	14	(15)	16	17	18	19	20
21	22	23	24	(25)	26	27	28	29	30
31	32	33	34	(35)	36	37	38	39	40
41	42	43	44	(45)	46	47	48	49	50
51	52	53	54	(55)	56	57	58	59	60
61	62	63	64	(65)	66	67	68	69	70
71	72	73	74	(75)	76	77	78	79	80
81	82	83	84	(85)	86	87	88	89	90
91	92	93	94	(95)	96	97	98	99	100

Exploring Tens with Bean Sticks

Children will enjoy making bean sticks and can use them for several activities. The procedure for making bean sticks is given.

1. Provide children with pinto or lima beans, glue, and craft sticks.

2. Have children count out 10 beans and glue them to a stick. Children continue until they have made nine 10-bean sticks. Ask children how they might count the beans without counting each bean separately. Children should suggest counting by tens, since there are 10 beans on each stick.

Now that the bean sticks have been made, have children try these activities:

- Children can practice counting by tens orally. Suggest that they take turns showing sticks to partners and skip-counting to find the total number of beans.

- Children can complete a function table, such as the one shown below, to indicate the relationship between the number of sticks and the total number of beans.

Bean Sticks	1	2	3	4	5	6	7	8	9
Number of Beans	(10)	(20)	(30)	(40)	(50)	(60)	(70)	(80)	(90)

© Judy/Instructo

J331001 Clearly Math • Grade 1

All About Numbers

Transparency 1

Use the *Hundred Chart* transparency to help children see the relationships between numbers as they solve and write riddles about two-digit numbers.

1. Read the following problem aloud and write it on the chalkboard:

   I am thinking of a number between 10 and 19. It is greater than 12. It is less than 18. If you add the digits, you get 7. What is the number? (16.)

2. Help children use the clues to solve the problem.

   a. To begin with, have them locate and identify the numbers between 10 and 19 and highlight them on the overhead projector.

   b. Ask a volunteer to read the next clue: "It is greater than 12." Invite a child to cross out 11 and 12 on the transparency. Ask a volunteer to read the next clue: "It is less than 18." Invite a child to cross out 18 and 19.

   c. Encourage children to use mental math to find the number among those left in which the sum of the digits is 7.

3. As an extension, have children make up riddles for their classmates to solve. After you have checked their riddles, allow the children time to share them with the class.

Number Webs

1. Assign each child a different two-digit number.

2. Have each child create a web showing every way in which he or she can think to represent his or her number. Responses will vary, but possible solutions could be similar to those shown in the following example.

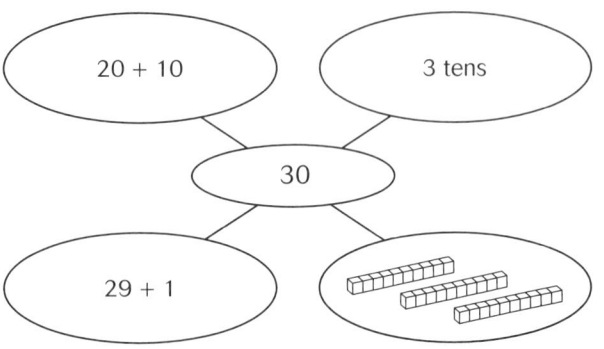

3. When children's webs are completed, interview the children so that they can tell you how they found their representations. Children should be able to show you on the hundred chart or with manipulatives how they arrived at the number of tens and ones, the pictorial representations, and so forth.

Dot-to-Dot Number Patterns

1. Give each child two sheets of paper. On one sheet, have children draw objects such as houses, trees, cars, or happy faces with simple lines.

2. Have children place the blank sheets of paper over their drawings. Children should look through to the drawings and draw dots on the top sheets, marking 10 locations along their outlines.

3. Have children draw dots labeled *Start* and then number the rest of the dots in increments of 1, 2, 5, or 10.

4. Have children exchange papers with classmates and complete each other's dot-to-dot pictures. Have children compare the completed dot-to-dots with the original pictures.

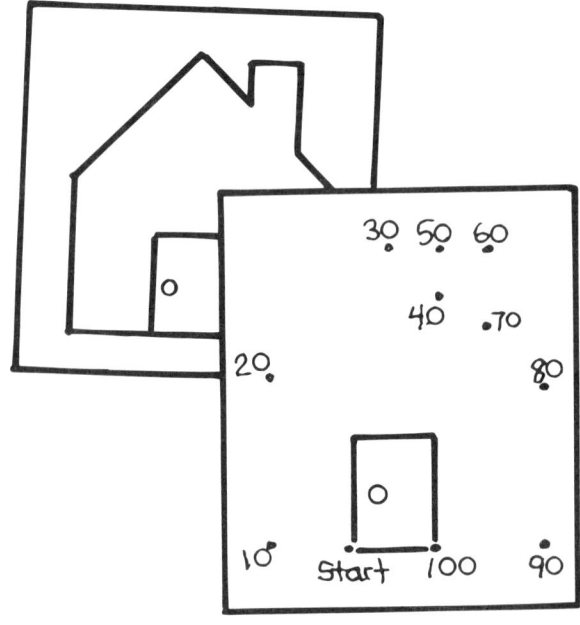

© Judy/Instructo

J331001 Clearly Math • Grade 1

Name _____ Numbers 1 to 10

Spin and Draw

You need

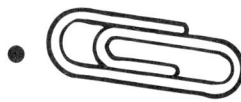 •

1. Make a spinner.
2. Spin it.
3. Draw and write a new number each time.

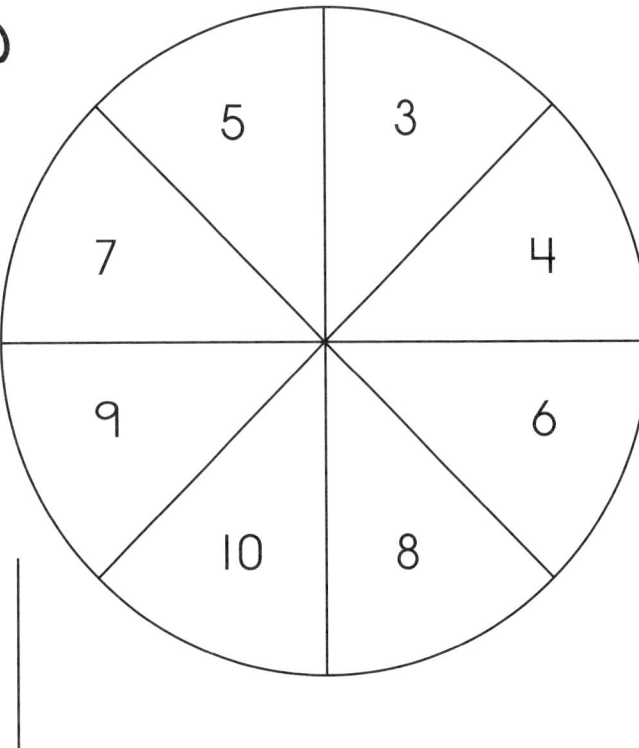

A.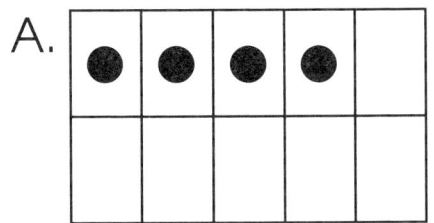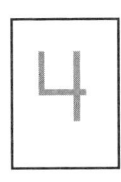

B.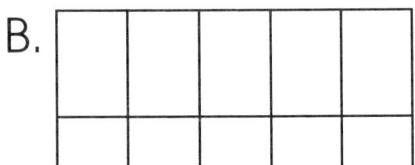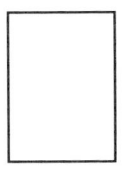

C.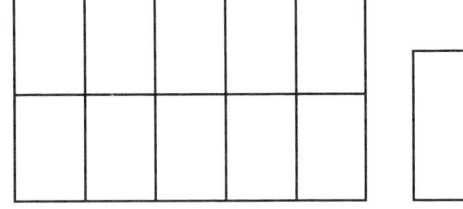

D.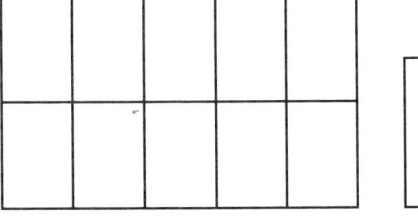

E.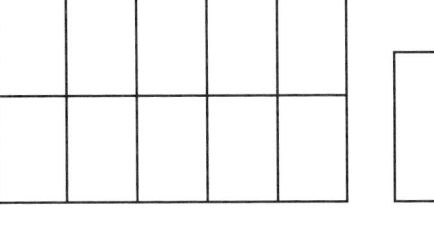

F.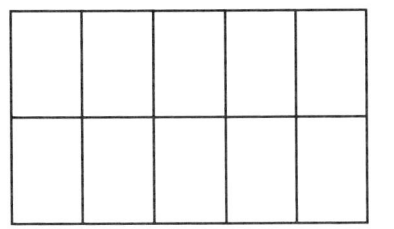

G.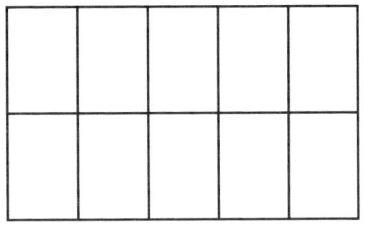

Teacher: Show students how to make a spinner by placing a paper clip at the center of the wheel and holding a pencil point inside the paper clip.

Name _____   Reading and Writing Two-Digit Numbers

Match Game

Match.

A.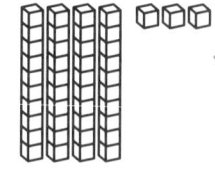

B.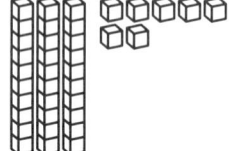

C.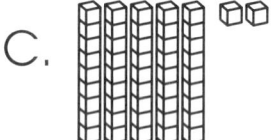

D.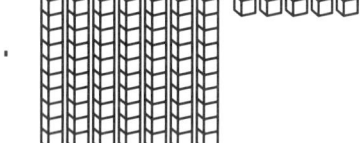

E.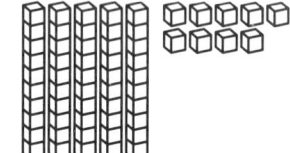

F.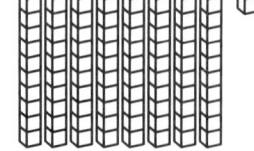

G.

tens	ones
3	7

75

tens	ones
7	5

43

tens	ones
4	3

52

tens	ones
5	2

37

tens	ones
8	1

18

tens	ones
1	8

59

tens	ones
5	9

81

© Judy/Instructo

Name _____   Comparing Numbers

A Greater Gator

Shade the box if it is true.

Look for a pattern.

10 < 9	26 < 30	19 > 91
90 > 78	44 < 34	17 < 81
26 > 29	15 < 19	20 < 19
30 > 32	92 < 95	81 > 89
83 < 75	27 > 24	62 < 49
58 < 60	19 > 20	29 > 21
56 > 85	18 > 16	79 > 81

Teacher: You may wish to display the *Hundred Chart* transparency and work as a class.

Name _____ Order, Skip-Counting by Fives

Follow the Dots

Start at the 0. End at 100.
Count by fives. Connect the dots.

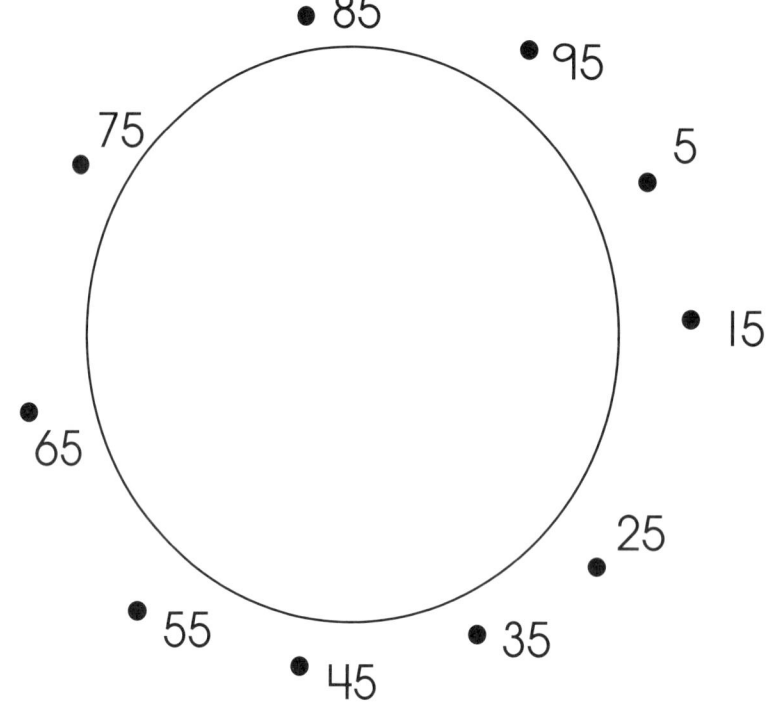

What is it? _____

Name _____   Number Patterns on **T1**
                                  a Hundred Chart

Up, Down, All Around

Use the *Hundred Chart* transparency.
Put your finger on the first number.
Move your finger ↑, ↓, →, or ←.
Write the number that you land on.

A. | 23 | → _24_ | 45 | → → ____

B. | 38 | ← ____ | 19 | ← ← ← ____

C. | 21 | ↓ ____ | 58 | ↓ ↓ ↓ ____

D. | 92 | ↑ ____ | 79 | ↑ ____

E. | 15 | ↓ ↓ ↓ ____ | 96 | ← ← ____

Circle the best one.

F. → means   +1   −1   +10   −10

G. ← means   +1   −1   +10   −10

H. ↓ means   +1   −1   +10   −10

I. ↑ means   +1   −1   +10   −10

Teacher: You may wish to work on this activity together with your class.

Addition

Sounds Good

Transparency 2

Display the 0–10 number line from the *Number Lines* transparency. You will need a glass jar and pennies or two-color counters.

1. Display the empty jar. Drop six pennies or counters, one at a time, into the jar while children watch. Tell them to focus on the number 6 on the number line and listen for an addition problem.

2. Move the jar so it is hidden from view and drop another penny in. Ask, "How many pennies are in the jar now?" (7.) "What makes you think so?" Children may respond that they heard more pennies being dropped into the jar. Display the jar, empty it in front of the class, and have a volunteer count the pennies to verify the sum. Ask, "What number sentence will tell what happened with the pennies in the jar?" (6 + 1 = 7.)

3. Invite a volunteer to show what happened with the pennies on the number line.

4. Repeat the activity, starting with 6 pennies and adding 2 more (6 + 2 = 8).

5. Continue as time and interest permit, changing the number of pennies with which to begin and the number you add.

Adding Up to a Number

Transparency 3

In this activity, children will find many ways to make the same number.

1. Reproduce the top portion of the *Ten-Frames and Two-Color Counters* transparency and distribute a copy to each child. Supply each child with 10 two-color counters.

2. Tell the children to count out 5 counters and place them red-side up on the top row of a ten-frame. Model this action on the overhead with the transparency and the red and yellow counters.

3. Ask the children to describe what they see (5 red counters and no yellow counters).

4. Write the number sentence 5 + 0 = 5 on the chalkboard and tell children that it represents their counters. Have the children record the number sentence on their papers.

5. Ask the children to flip one counter over and say a number sentence to describe what they see (4 + 1 = 5). Add the number sentence to the first one on the chalkboard and have the children record it on their papers.

6. Have children turn another counter over and repeat the process (3 + 2 = 5). Continue until all the counters are yellow-side up and the children have a collection of number sentences.

   (Note: You may wish to call attention to number sentences that have the same addends in a different order, such as 4 + 1 = 5 and 1 + 4 = 5.)

7. Repeat the procedure for numbers 6 through 10, having the children model the ways to make numbers and listing number sentences.

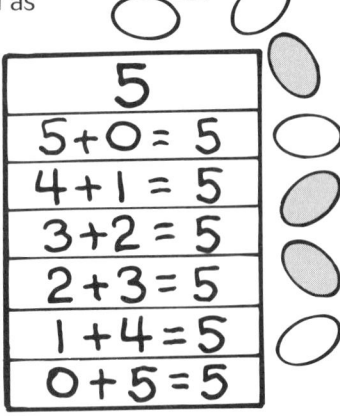

Commutative Cubes

This simple activity helps children see the commutative property of addition.

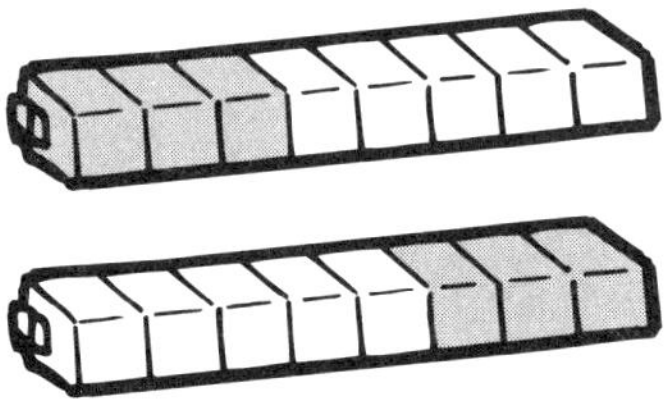

1. Provide each child with up to five connecting cubes in each of two different colors.

2. Have the children make a 3-train of one color and a 5-train of another.

3. Tell the children to combine trains in 3-to-5 order and to give the sum (8). Write $3 + 5 = 8$ on the board.

4. Have the children turn their trains over so that the 5-train comes first.

5. Ask, "Do you think there are still a total of 8 cubes? Why or why not?" Have the children count the cubes to verify their predictions. Write $5 + 3 = 8$ on the chalkboard beneath the first sentence.

6. Repeat the procedure a few more times with different number pairs, such as $2 + 4 = 6$ and $4 + 2 = 6$, $4 + 5 = 9$ and $5 + 4 = 9$, and so on.

7. Ask the children what they have found out about the order of the addends in an addition sentence (the sum stays the same regardless of the order).

Sums with Ten-Frames

Transparency 3

1. Reproduce the *Ten-Frames and Two-Color Counters* transparency and distribute a copy to each child. Supply each child with 18 two-color counters.

2. Have the children place eight counters red-side up on the top ten-frame.

3. Have the children place three counters yellow-side up on the bottom ten-frame.

4. Ask, "What addition 'phrase' describes the two sets of counters?" ($8 + 3$.)

5. Ask the children to combine the sets by moving enough yellow counters to fill the top ten-frame, then leaving the "leftover" counters in the bottom ten frame.

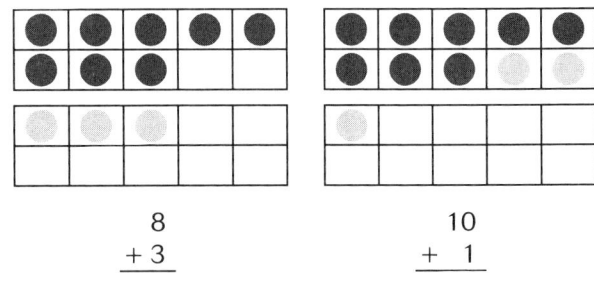

$$\begin{array}{r} 8 \\ + 3 \\ \hline \end{array} \qquad \begin{array}{r} 10 \\ + 1 \\ \hline \end{array}$$

6. Ask the children how many counters there are in all (11). Have the children complete their number sentences so they read $8 + 3 = 11$. Say, "Can anyone name another number sentence that describes the counters?" Encourage the children to see that $8 + 3 = 10 + 1$, since counters were moved to fill a ten-frame.

7. Repeat the procedure for $8 + 7$ (15) and $7 + 6$ (13). Continue as interest permits.

Author, Author!

Knowledge of addition concepts can be assessed by having children formulate and solve original problems.

1. Provide each child with a different addition "phrase" with a sum up to 18. Examples include $6 + 3 = ?$, $5 + 5 = ?$, $4 + 7 = ?$, and $6 + 8 = ?$

2. Have children write story problems with the addition phrases they were given. Then have them find the solutions.

3. Allow time for children to share their stories and solutions with the class. Check to make sure that the story problems match the number "phrases," and that the solutions are correct. Ask the children to tell how they solved the problems. (Answers may include counting on, using models, drawing and counting pictures, and mental math.)

Name _____ Sums up to 10

Colorful Sums

Add. Color.
  5 red   6 orange   7 yellow
  8 green   9 blue   10 purple

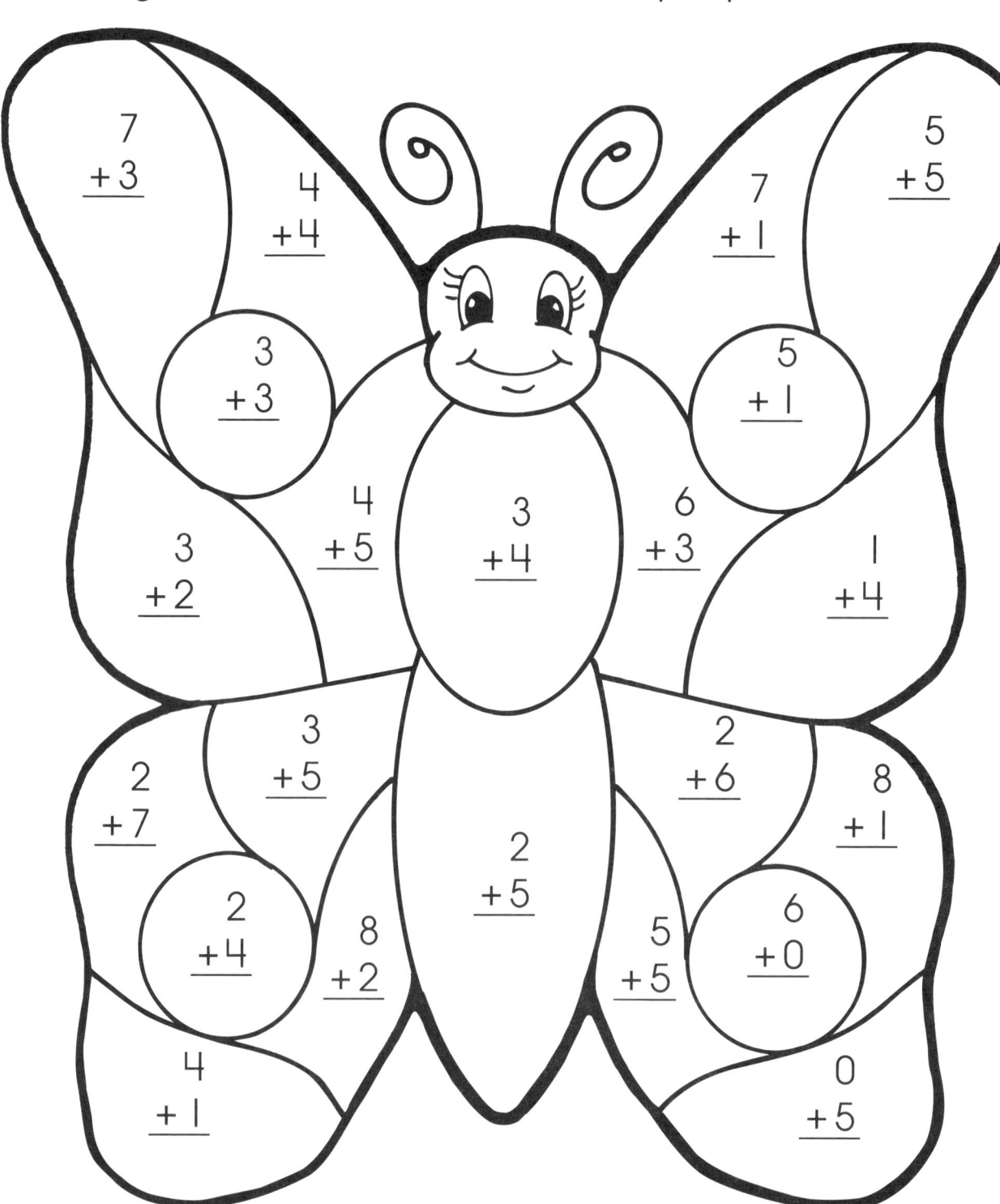

Name _____ Making a Ten

Secret Message

Solve the problems.
Match your answers with the pictures 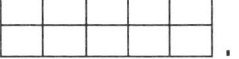.
Write the letters in the spaces below.
Read the secret message.

1. 8 + 6 = ☐   9 + 3 = ☐   7 + 4 = ☐

2. 6 + 9 = ☐   7 + 6 = ☐   9 + 9 = ☐

3. 8 + 9 = ☐   9 + 7 = ☐   8 + 5 = ☐

4. 3 + 8 = ☐   1 + 9 = ☐   7 + 8 = ☐

A   E   C   I   T

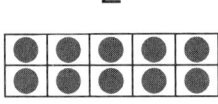 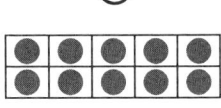 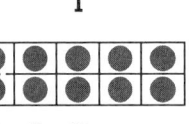 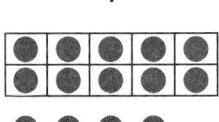

S   N   P   L

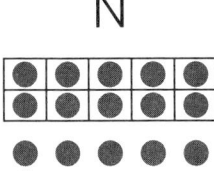 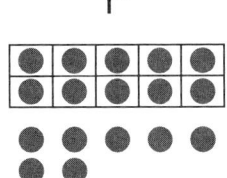 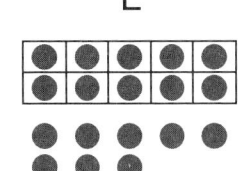

___ ___ ___   ___ ___
 14 11 16   13 15

___ ___ ___ ___ ___ ___ ___
 15 17 11 12 13 10 18

© Judy/Instructo   J331001 Clearly Math • Grade 1

Name _____ Using Doubles to Add

Drawing Doubles

Draw the double in the circle.
Then find the sum.

A.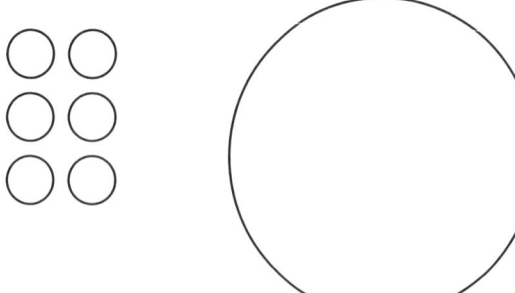

6 + ☐ = ☐

B.

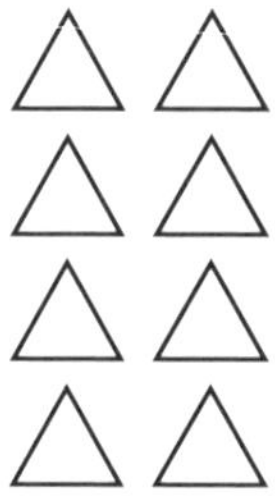

△ △
△ △
△ △
△ △

◯

8 + ☐ = ☐

C.

♡ ♡
♡ ♡
♡ ♡
♡

◯

7 + ☐ = ☐

D.

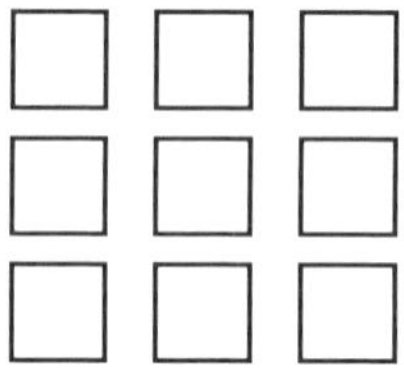

☐☐☐
☐☐☐
☐☐☐

◯

9 + ☐ = ☐

Add the doubles + 1.
Use the doubles to help.

E. 6 + 6 = ☐, so 6 + 7 = ☐.

F. 7 + 7 = ☐, so 7 + 8 = ☐.

G. 8 + 8 = ☐, so 8 + 9 = ☐.

H. 9 + 9 = ☐, so 9 + 10 = ☐.

© Judy/Instructo   16 Reproducible   J331001 Clearly Math • Grade 1

Name _____   Practice Facts to 18

Mix 'n' Match

Draw lines to match.

8 + 4	15	10 + 1
6 + 9	13	10 + 2
7 + 6	12	10 + 5
2 + 9	11	10 + 3
5 + 9	16	10 + 8
8 + 8	18	10 + 7
8 + 9	14	10 + 4
9 + 9	17	10 + 6

© Judy/Instructo   17 Reproducible   J331001 Clearly Math • Grade 1

Name _____ Problem Solving with Addition **T4**

Shop for Stickers

Shop at the Sticker Store.
Write a number sentence.
Tell how much in all.

A.

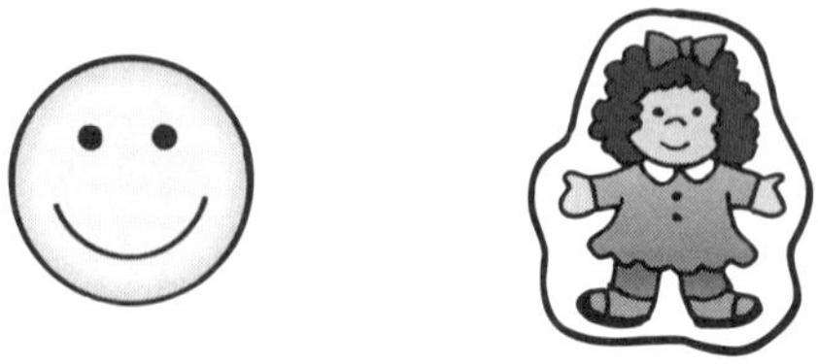

___3___ ¢ + ___8___ ¢ = ___11___ ¢

B.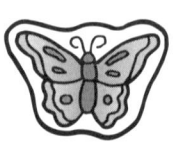

_____ ¢ + _____ ¢ = _____ ¢

C.

_____ ¢ + _____ ¢ = _____ ¢

D.

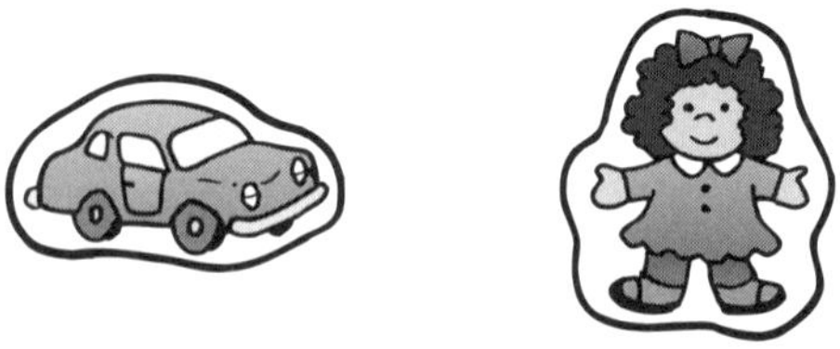

_____ ¢ + _____ ¢ = _____ ¢

E.

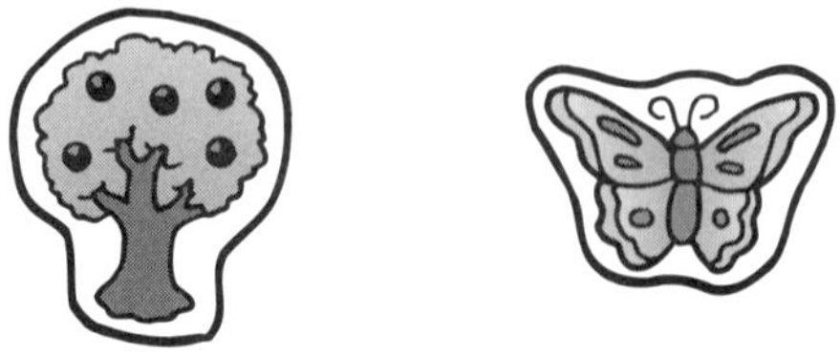

_____ ¢ + _____ ¢ = _____ ¢

F.

_____ ¢ + _____ ¢ = _____ ¢

G.

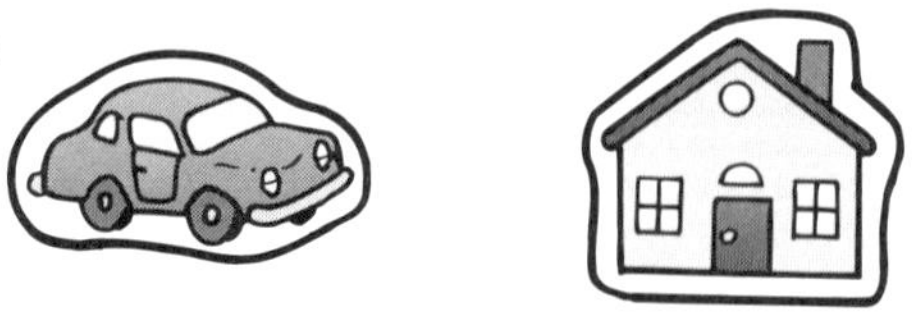

_____ ¢ + _____ ¢ = _____ ¢

H.

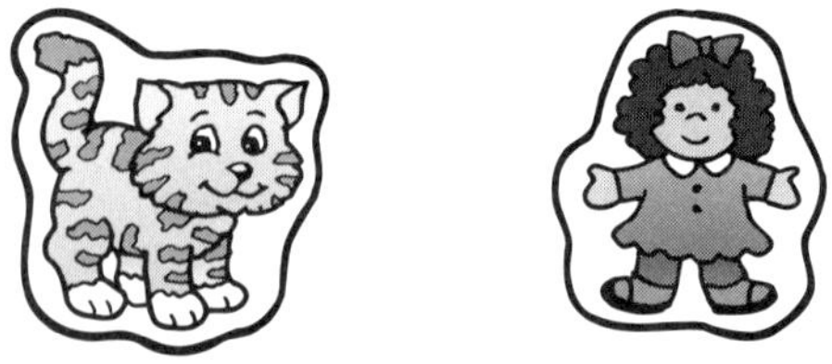

_____ ¢ + _____ ¢ = _____ ¢

I. Draw what you want.
   Tell how much it will cost.

Teacher: Display the *Sticker Store* transparency for this activity page.

Name _____   Adding One- and Two-Digit Numbers

B-I-N-G-O

Add. Shade the box with the sum.
Draw a line to show the B-I-N-G-O!

A.	19 + 3	26 + 3	88 + 2	12 + 6	37 + 5
B.	45 + 5	52 + 3	79 + 2	28 + 4	51 + 7
C.	75 + 7	68 + 1	57 + 3	32 + 5	93 + 2
D.	48 + 4	53 + 3	64 + 6	90 + 4	72 + 8

B	I	N	G	O
22	56	20	82	18
32	29	12	70	69
14	58	60	90	94
50	13	37	80	81
52	95	42	55	10

© Judy/Instructo

19 Reproducible

J331001 Clearly Math • Grade 1

SUBTRACTION

Subtract to Compare

In this activity, have children work in pairs to explore comparing two amounts.

1. Provide each pair of children with two different-colored 10-trains of connecting cubes.

2. Direct each child to make his or her train a different length than that of his or her partner.

3. Tell the students to align their trains along the left edges. Ask them to determine which train is longer, and by how many cubes.

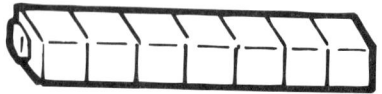

4. Have the pairs of children write number sentences that describe the difference between the lengths of their cube trains.

5. Ask pairs of children to switch partners and have them repeat the activity. You may wish to provide variety by having children find which train is shorter, and by how many cubes.

Subtraction on a Number Line

Transparency 2

Using walk-on number lines helps children relate to the concept of subtraction, or counting back. After several attempts, they can easily apply what they learn to a smaller version of the same model. Reproduce and distribute the 0–10 number line from the *Number Lines* transparency to each child.

1. Use masking tape to construct a large, walk-on number line on the classroom floor.

2. Write a number sentence, such as 7 – 1, on the chalkboard.

3. Ask a volunteer to come to the front of the room and model the sentence on the number line. Invite the class to help the volunteer. Ask questions like "Where should _____ stand to begin to solve this sentence? How do you know?" or "Once _____ is at the starting point, how many steps and in which direction should he/she move? Why does that make sense?"

4. Invite the class to give the answer, or difference (6).

5. Repeat the procedure for several other subtraction examples.

6. When the children are comfortable with the concept and procedure of subtracting on the number line, have them use their own number lines to find differences for examples such as 10 – 2, 9 – 3, 8 – 1, and 10 – 4.

Number Webs

Have the children write all the ways in which they can think to show numbers between 11 and 20 with addition and subtraction facts on number webs. Display finished products on a bulletin board or along a classroom wall. An example is shown for the number 13.

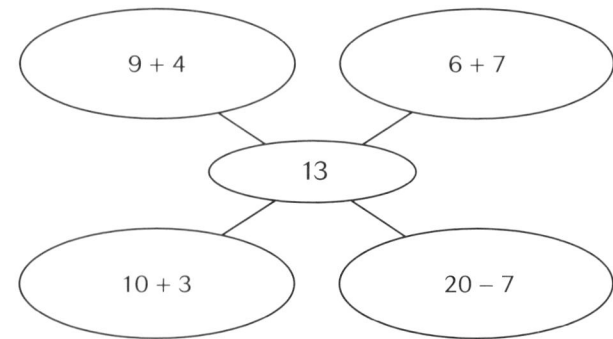

© Judy/Instructo   20   J331001 Clearly Math • Grade 1

Relating Addition and Subtraction

Children can use finger play to explore the relationship between addition and subtraction.

1. Have each child hold up three fingers on one hand and two fingers on the other.

2. Ask the children how many fingers they are holding up in all (5).

3. Invite volunteers to say a number sentence that describes their fingers (3 + 2 = 5).

4. Tell the children to cross their arms at the elbows so that they are looking at their fingers in reverse order. Ask the children to give a new number sentence that describes their fingers (2 + 3 = 5).

5. Next, have each child hide the hand showing two fingers behind his or her back. Say, "You had five fingers up in all. You took two fingers away. How many fingers are left?" (3.)

6. Ask a volunteer to say a number sentence that describes his or her fingers (5 − 2 = 3).

7. Have each child bring the hand showing two fingers back to the front, so that five fingers show again. This time, have each child put the hands showing three fingers behind his or her back. Ask children to give a number sentence that describes their fingers (5 − 3 = 2).

8. Repeat the process with other addends, minuends, and subtrahends. When the children feel familiar with the relationship between addition and subtraction, have them describe orally or in writing how they think a "fact family" got its name. Ask them to be specific, using the 3, 6, 9 fact family as an example. You may wish to encourage children to draw pictures to clarify their responses.

(Answers will vary. Responses should include ideas such as: Fact families [excluding those with doubles] have two addition sentences, where two parts are combined to make the third, and two subtraction sentences, where one part is removed from the second, leaving the third. All four number sentences use the same numbers.)

Write It Yourself

1. Provide each child with a different subtraction "phrase" with a minuend no higher than 18. Examples include 8 − 3, 10 − 2, 11 − 5, 13 − 5, and 16 − 9.

2. Have the children write story problems with the subtraction phrases they were given. Then have them find the solutions.

3. Allow the children time to share their stories and solutions with the class. Check to make sure that the story problems match the number "phrases," and that the solutions are correct. Ask children to tell how they solved the problems. (Answers may include counting on, using models, drawing and counting pictures, and mental math.)

© Judy/Instructo   J331001 Clearly Math • Grade 1

Which Operation?

In order for children to be successful problem solvers, they need to be able to make plans. This activity helps children decide which operations should be used in the planning stages of solving problems. Finding the actual solutions to these problems is not necessary. Use this activity throughout the year to ensure that the children have a conceptual understanding of the uses of each operation with regard to problem solving.

1. Supply each child with two index cards. Ask him or her to make a plus sign (+) on one card and a minus (−) sign on the other card. Encourage the children to make their signs large and clear, so that you can see all their cards at a glance.

2. Tell the following story: "Mac and Jill have a toy car collection. Mac has 7 cars. Jill has 5 cars. If they put their collections together, how many cars would they have?"

3. Ask the children to hold up the cards that show how they would solve the problem. Check to make sure that children chose addition. Ask, "Why does it make sense to use addition to solve the problem?" The children should be able to explain that addition is called for because sets are being combined.

4. Repeat for these stories: "Mrs. Green bought 3 pounds of red apples and 8 pounds of green apples. How many more pounds of green apples than red apples did Mrs. Green buy?" (Subtraction; two amounts are being compared.) "Hector has 9¢. He spends 5¢ on a rubber ball. How much money does Hector have after he pays for the ball?" (Subtraction; some money is being spent, or taken away.)

5. Continue to make up story problems as time and interest permit, challenging the children to show their operation cards and explain their thinking.

Half the Group

1. Write *12 − 6* on the chalkboard. Ask various children to tell how they would solve the problem.

2. Invite 12 volunteers to come to the front of the room. Tap 6 of the children and have them stand aside. Point out that the number of children standing aside is the same as the number of children still standing at the front of the room.

3. Ask, "Which addition double could help you solve the subtraction problem?" (6 + 6)

4. Invite seated volunteers to stand and write *12 − 6 = 6* and *6 + 6 = 12* on the chalkboard. Encourage the children to compare the sentences. The children should observe that both sentences use the numbers 6 and 12, that 6 is used twice in the addition sentence, and that 6 represents the part taken away and the part remaining in the subtraction sentence.

5. Repeat the activity with other doubles to help children become familiar with the relationships between doubles facts for addition and subtraction.

Name _____   Differences from 10 or Less

Color the Differences

Subtract. Color.
- 3 red
- 6 green
- 4 orange
- 7 blue
- 5 yellow
- 8 purple

Name _____   Differences from 18 or Less

Magic Subtraction Squares

Subtract → and ↓.

A.

16	7	9
8	1	
8		

B.

13	5	
4	0	

C.

18	9	
10	2	

D.

15	6	
9	3	

E.

17	9	
8	7	

F. Make your own!

14		

Name _____   Missing Addends

In the Bag

How many in the bag?
Draw them.
Write how many.

A.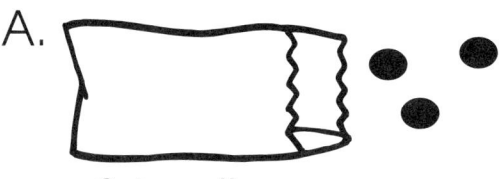
8 in all.
___ in the bag.

B.
7 in all.
___ in the bag.

C.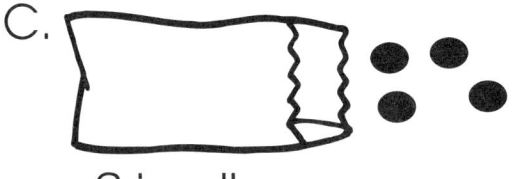
9 in all.
___ in the bag.

D.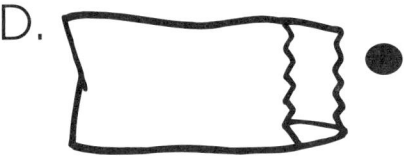
6 in all.
___ in the bag.

E.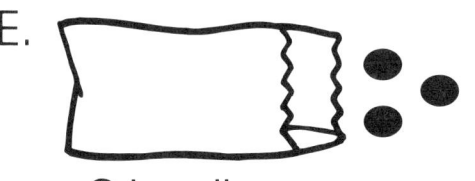
9 in all.
___ in the bag.

F.
6 in all.
___ in the bag.

G.
8 in all.
___ in the bag.

H.
10 in all.
___ in the bag.

I. How did you know how many to draw in each bag?

_____

© Judy/Instructo   J331001 Clearly Math • Grade 1

Name _____ Problem Solving with Subtraction **T4**

Compare Costs

Shop at the Sticker Store.
Circle the one that costs more.
Tell how much more.
Write a number sentence.

A.

_5_ ¢ – _3_ ¢ = _2_ ¢
more

B.

___ ¢ – ___ ¢ = ___ ¢
more

C.

___ ¢ – ___ ¢ = ___ ¢
more

D.

___ ¢ – ___ ¢ = ___ ¢
more

E.

___ ¢ – ___ ¢ = ___ ¢
more

F.

___ ¢ – ___ ¢ = ___ ¢
more

Circle the answer.

G. Which costs 2¢ less than 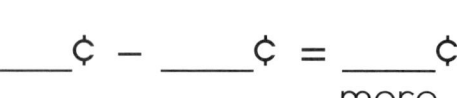?

H. Which costs 5¢ less than ?

Name _____ Fact Families

Dot's My Family!

Draw dots on the dominoes.
Write fact families to show what you draw.

A. 10 dots in all.

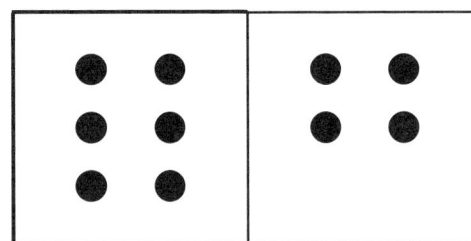

__6__ + __4__ = __10__

___ + __6__ = ___

___ − __6__ = ___

___ − ___ = __6__

B. 12 dots in all.

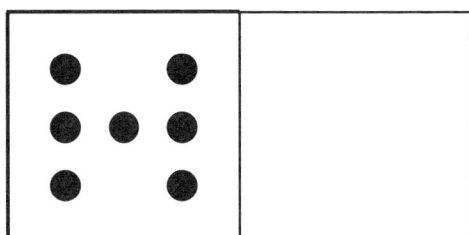

__7__ + ___ = __12__

___ + ___ = ___

___ − ___ = ___

___ − ___ = ___

C. 13 dots in all.

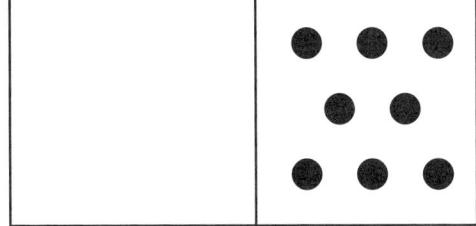

___ + ___ = ___

___ + ___ = ___

___ − ___ = ___

___ − ___ = ___

D. 15 dots in all.

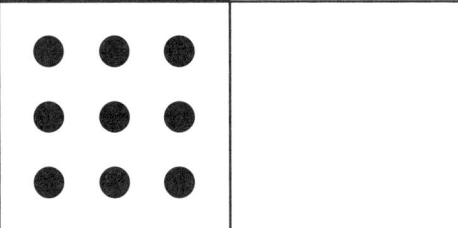

___ + ___ = ___

___ + ___ = ___

___ − ___ = ___

___ − ___ = ___

© Judy/Instructo Reproducible J331001 Clearly Math • Grade 1

Name _____ Choose the Operation

Follow the Path

Follow the path. Circle **+** or **−**.
Write the missing numbers.

A Cross-Number Puzzle

Subtracting One-Digit from Two-Digit Numbers

Read the clues.
Write the numbers in the puzzle.

Across

A. 53 – 3 = ___
B. 80 – 3 = ___
C. 21 – 8 = ___
E. 44 – 5 = ___
F. 70 – 7 = ___
G. 20 – 7 = ___
H. 65 – 5 = ___
I. 29 – 4 = ___
J. 13 – 5 = ___
K. 46 + 4 = ___

Down

A. 58 – 1 = ___
B. 79 – 6 = ___
C. 22 – 3 = ___
D. 21 – 8 = ___
E. 38 – 5 = ___
F. 68 – 8 = ___
G. 11 – 1 = ___
H. 71 – 6 = ___
I. 29 – 9 = ___
J. 90 – 8 = ___

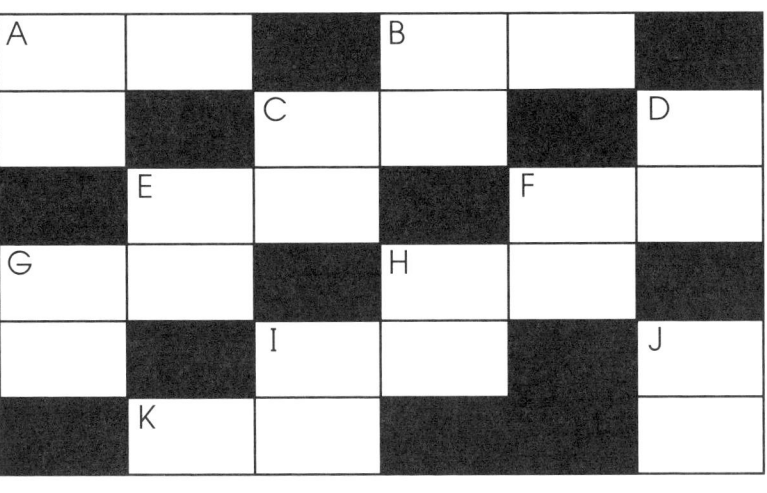

Geometry and Fractions

Face Trace

1. Provide groups of children with 8½" x 11" sheets of paper and a collection of classroom objects, such as chalkboard erasers, tissue boxes, masking tape rolls, and plastic tops. If you have no classroom objects with triangular faces, simply provide each group of children with a geometric solid pyramid.

2. Ask the groups of children to identify the geometric shape of each object. For example, they may say that a tissue box is a cube, a masking tape roll is a cylinder, and so forth.

3. Show the children how to place the face of an object on a sheet of paper and trace around it. Allow the children time to trace around as many faces as they can for each figure. (Boxes may have two or three different-size faces to trace; cylinders will have only one.)

4. When tracing is completed, have the groups of children place all their face traces and objects in the center of their workspaces. Have the groups switch places. Challenge them to try to match each face trace with the figure from which it was made.

I Spy

This fun game reinforces geometric vocabulary and concepts.

1. Review the following terms: *curves, faces, edges, corners, space*.

2. Place several objects on a table or desk in the front of the room (for example, chalk, a ball, and a tissue box).

3. Ask a volunteer to describe one of the objects with the words *corner, face,* and *curves* without saying which object it is. For example, the child may say, "I spy with my little eye an object that has no faces or corners. What do I spy?" (A ball.)

4. Ask the child's classmates to identify the object and its shape.

5. Replace the object with the others and repeat the activity as time and interest permit.

Same Size and Shape

In this game, children will use verbal clues to help their partners make congruent shapes.

1. Reproduce the dot paper (page 52) and distribute one sheet to each child.

2. Arrange children in pairs. Have one child in each pair make a figure on dot paper without showing his or her partner.

3. Have the children describe the figure to their partners. Descriptions should include the number of sides and the number of "dots" that are touched to form each side. The partners should try to draw the figures that are described to them.

4. Have children compare the shapes to see if they are congruent. (Location on the dot paper grid is not important.)

5. Have players switch roles and repeat the activity.

Pattern Block Equal Parts

Transparency 5

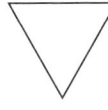

1. Have children work in pairs. Display the *Pattern Block Design* transparency and distribute a copy of the *Pattern Blocks* reproducible (page 53) to each child. Ask children to color the pattern blocks as they appear on the transparency and then to cut them into separate shapes. You may wish to have parent volunteers help with this.

2. Ask one child in each pair to place one blue diamond pattern block in front of his or her partner.

3. Challenge the children's partners to find two other blocks that, when joined, match the diamond in size and shape (green triangles).

4. Have the first child in each pair place two triangles on top of the diamond to verify that they are two equal halves. Guide the children to discover that each part or triangle is one half the size of the diamond. Ask a volunteer to verify this with pieces on the overhead projector.

5. Have partners switch roles. This time, have the children work with the red trapezoid. Ask how many triangles would be needed to match the size and shape of the trapezoid. Children should verify and observe that three are needed, and that each triangle represents one third of the trapezoid.

6. When the children are familiar with the concept of equal parts and fractions, have them work independently. Challenge each child to use the pattern blocks and find the fractional part of the yellow hexagon covered by a red trapezoid (one half), a blue diamond (one third), and a green triangle (one sixth). Invite the children to glue or trace the pieces to show their work, and to explain

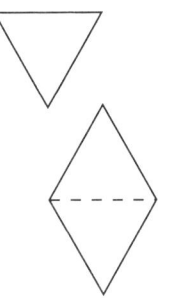

in writing how they got their answers. (Children may say that they placed the trapezoids on top of the hexagons and found that two were needed to fit exactly; since two were needed, each piece was 1 out of 2, or $1/2$, of the shape.)

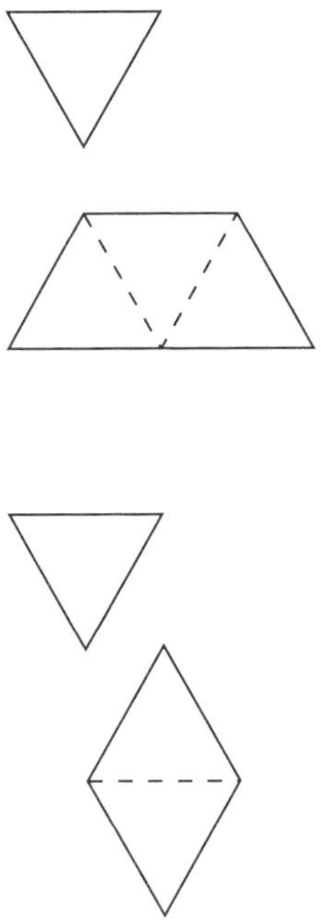

Painted Symmetry

Children will enjoy learning about symmetry with this activity. Each child will need two half-sheets of construction paper and acrylic or tempera paint.

1. Have each child fold one sheet of construction paper in half; then unfold it.

2. Ask each child to paint the picture of his or her choice on one half of the sheet. While the paint is still wet have the children fold their sheets along the original folds and press.

3. Have children unfold their sheets and describe what they see (the same picture appears on both sides of the fold). Invite volunteers to explain that the fold line divides the entire picture into two halves that are mirror images.

4. Ask children to predict what would happen if they tried the same thing again with new sheets of paper (two mirror images of the same picture would again result).

5. Once children have made their predictions, have them fold and unfold the second half-sheets of paper and paint more pictures.

Name _____ Attributes of Solid Shapes

Cross Out

One shape does not belong.

Write the letter of that shape at the bottom of the page.

Then cross out the shape.

1.

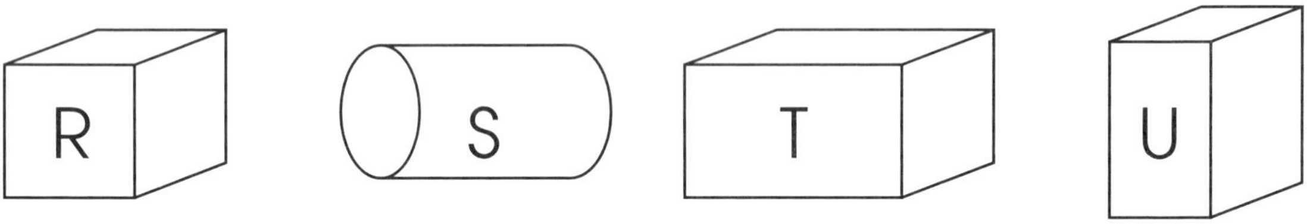

2.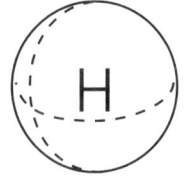

3.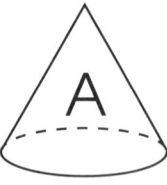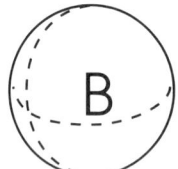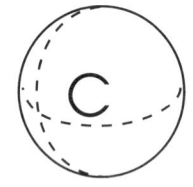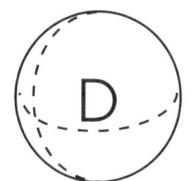

4.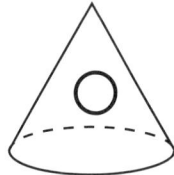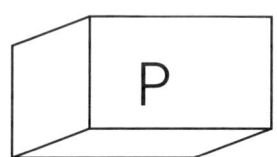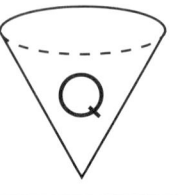

5.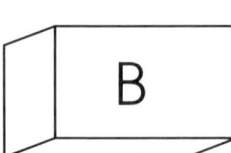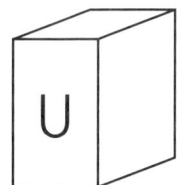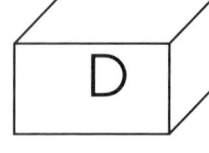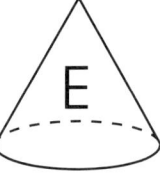

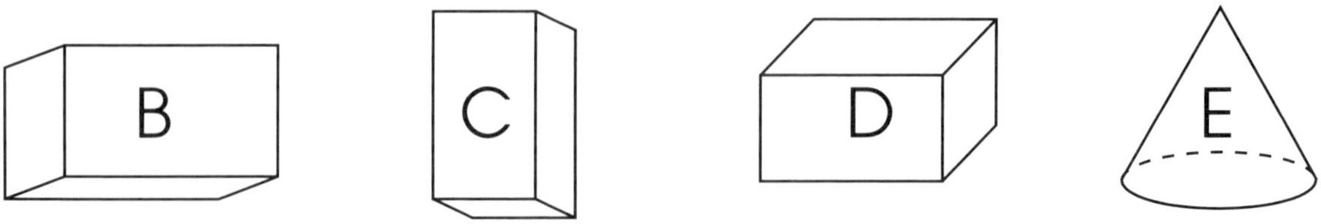

___ ___ ___ ___ ___
 1   2   3   4   5

What is the secret word? _____

© Judy/Instructo   32 Reproducible   J331001 Clearly Math • Grade 1

Name _____   Attributes of Plane Shapes

Color by Shape

Color.

▭ red   ○ yellow   △ green   ☐ blue

How many  ▭ ? ____   How many △ ? ____ 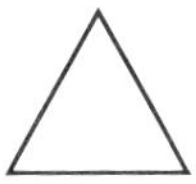
How many ☐ ? ____   How many ○ ? ____

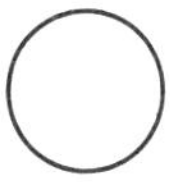

Name _____ Symmetry

Matching Halves

Which have two matching halves?

Draw a line through each to show them.

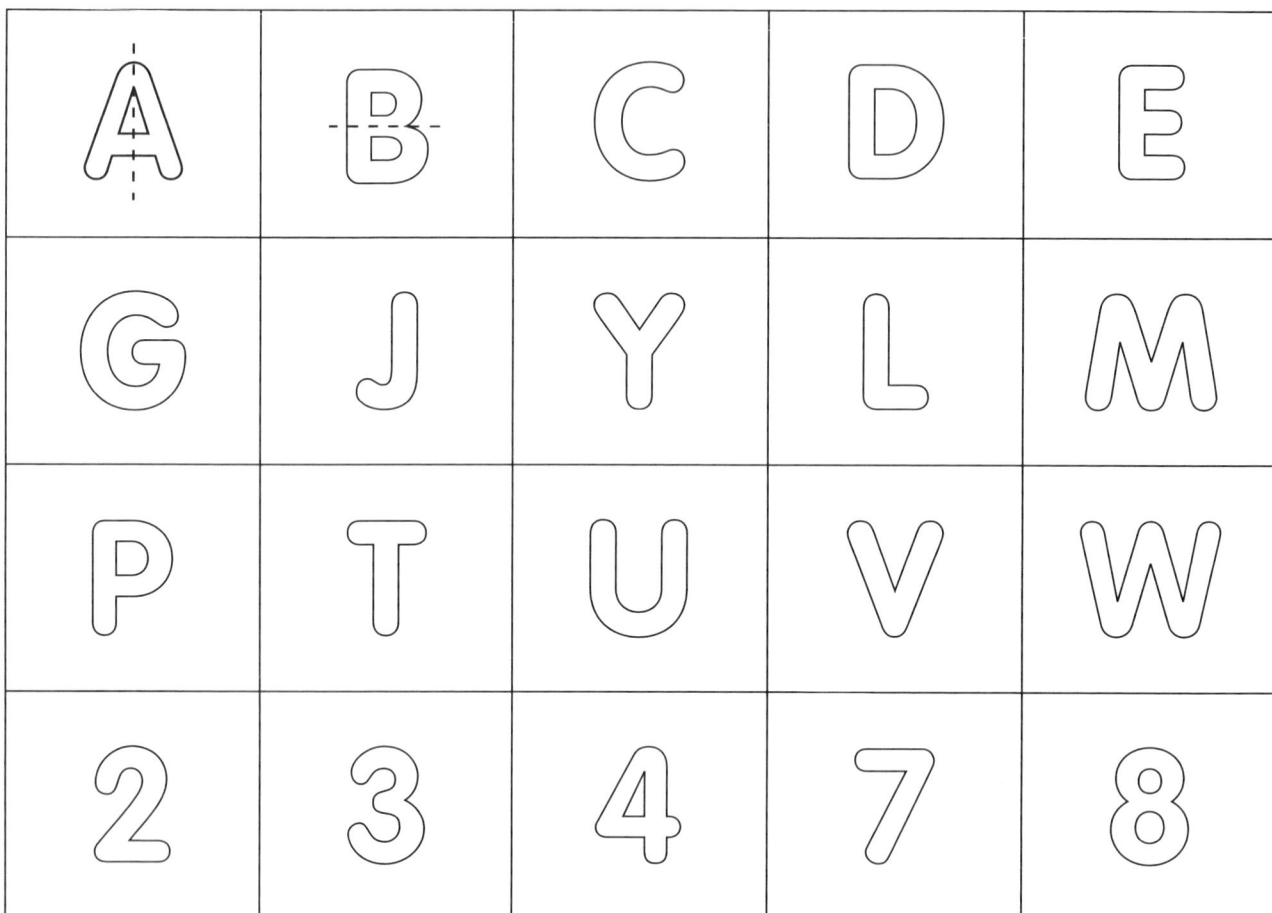

Write your name in capital letters.

Draw lines through the letters that show matching halves.

Name _____   Identifying Halves, Thirds, and Fourths

Fraction Path

A. Which shapes show $\frac{1}{2}$? Draw a path.

B. Which shapes show $\frac{1}{3}$? Draw a path.

C. Which shapes show $\frac{1}{4}$? Draw a path.

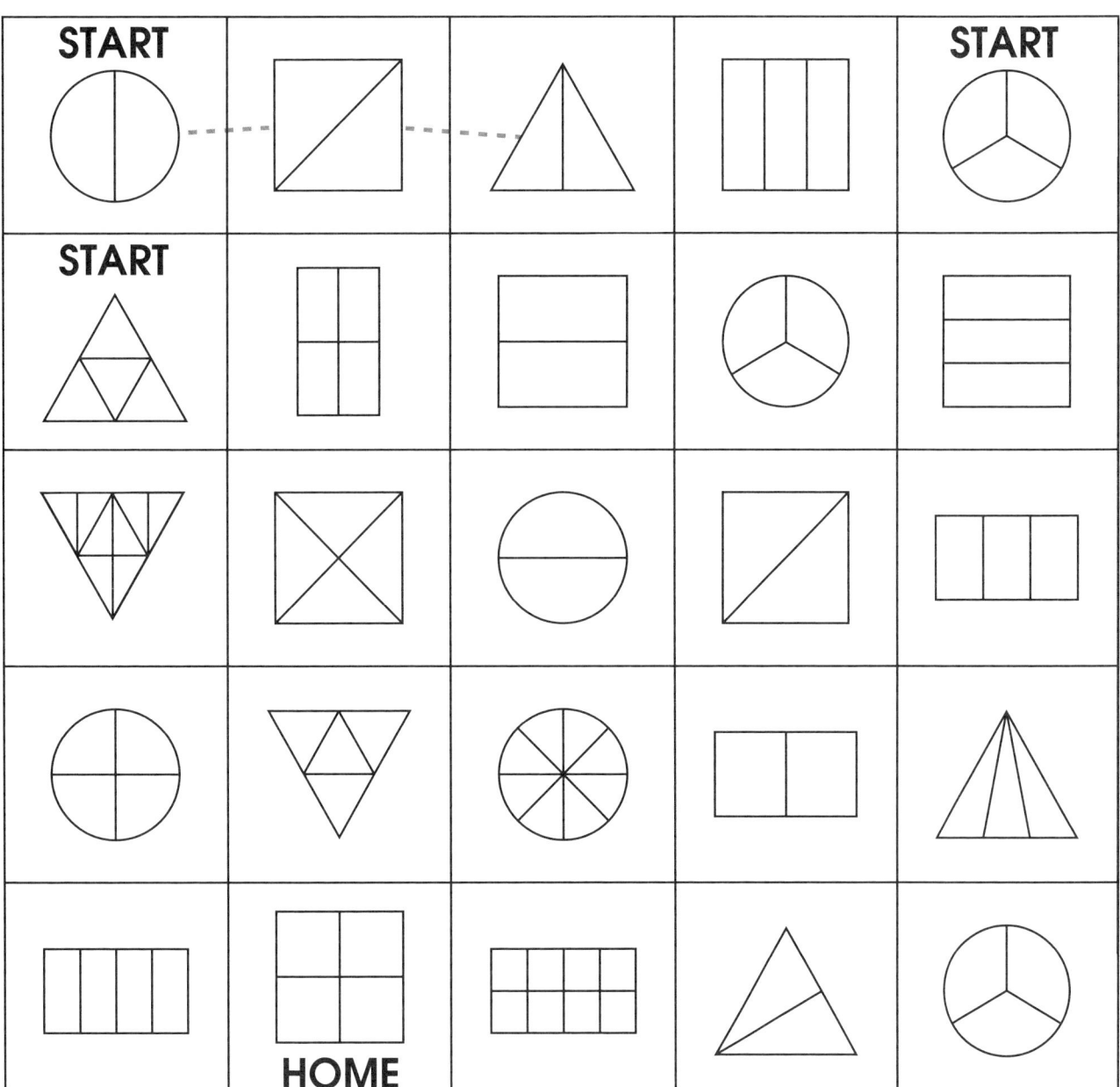

Which path goes home? $\frac{1}{2}$ $\frac{1}{3}$ $\frac{1}{4}$

Time, Measurement, and Money

Units of Time

1. Ask the children to listen to each activity you describe and tell you whether it takes closer to one minute or one hour to complete. You may wish to include the following activities:

   Erase the chalkboard (minute).

   Count to 100 (minute).

   Watch a television program (hour).

   Bake a cake (hour).

   Wash your hands (minute).

   Play a game of soccer (hour).

   Watch a circus (hour).

2. Ask one child at a time to describe an activity. Ask the class to listen and say whether they think the activity takes closer to one minute or one hour to complete.

3. As an extension, you may have children suggest activities that could be completed in a matter of minutes or hours. For minutes, children may suggest eating lunch and reading a story. For hours, children may suggest going to school and sleeping.

A Day in the Life

Transparency 6

ACU

1. Engage the children in a discussion about what they do during the day. They may mention activities such as waking up, eating breakfast, going to school, attending music lessons, going to soccer practice, eating dinner, watching television, reading a book, and going to bed. Using the children's suggestions, create a master list on the chalkboard or overhead.

2. Display the *Judy Clock* transparency. Ask volunteers to "set" the clock to show the time of day at which each activity on the list may occur.

3. Distribute several sheets of plain paper to each child. Ask the children to use one sheet as title pages for books about their days, entitled "___'s Day."

4. On the other pages, have the children draw simple clock faces (large circles with the numbers 1–12 in their proper locations). Then have the children draw hands on each clock to represent the time of day when they begin a specific activity. Below each clock, have them write a caption describing the activity and write the digital time.

5. When the children have completed their books, have them review them with you. Ask children to put the activities in the order in which they occur throughout the day. When you have finished reviewing and evaluating the children's work, have them staple the pages together to complete the books.

6. Have the children place the completed books in a location where classmates can read them.

© Judy/Instructo

J331001 Clearly Math • Grade 1

Measuring by Direct Comparison

1. Review comparative measurement terms such as *taller, longer,* and *shorter* with children. Ask a volunteer to stand beside you. Ask the class, "Who is taller?" (Answers may vary.)

2. From their seats, have the children name things in the classroom that they think are shorter than they are. Create a master list on the blackboard under the heading *Shorter Than Me.* Repeat for items that are taller and list them under an appropriate heading.

3. Have the children examine their own hand spans. Then ask them to name classroom objects that they think are shorter than their hand spans. Ask children how they might test their predictions (hold their hand spans against the objects).

4. Allow the children ample time to work in small groups and test their predictions, recording their findings on paper. Discuss results as a class.

Measure Treasure Hunt

Children will be able to estimate measurements after performing this fun activity.

1. Have children work in groups of four. Provide each group with cube trains of 1-cube, 2-cube, 5-cube, and 10-cube length. Each student in the group should use a different cube train.

2. Have the children try to find items around the classroom whose lengths are close to the length of the cube trains they are holding. For example, a child with the 1-cube train may find that a paper clip is about the length of his or her cube train. Encourage group members to help each other find objects that are the lengths of their trains. Allow them ample time to complete the activity.

3. As a class, discuss results. Create a master list for each cube-train length and have children contribute their findings.

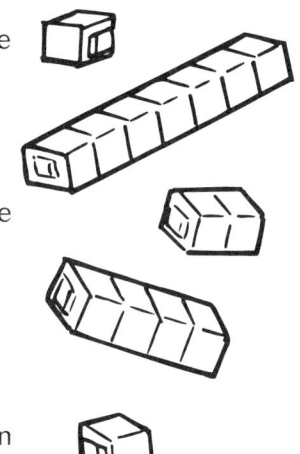

Body Measure

1. Provide pairs of children with a centimeter ruler and two plain sheets of paper.

2. Have children in each pair draw stick figures representing themselves. Make sure children's pictures include arms, hands, legs, feet, heads, and ears.

3. Have children in each pair take turns measuring each other's body parts and recording the results. For example, one child measures his or her partner's arms. Once the measurement is made, the child records the result on his or her partner's stick-figure picture. Partners switch roles and repeat.

4. Discuss the findings as a class. Ask the children to tell, for example, how long their arms are. Record children's responses on the chalkboard. Repeat for leg lengths. Ask children what they observe. (Legs are longer than arms.) Repeat for feet, heads, and ears.

Sorting Coins

Transparency 7

1. Display an assortment of overhead coins from the *Rulers and Coins* transparency. Draw two lines on the overhead projector to create a four-section grid. Label the sections *Penny 1¢, Nickel 5¢, Dime 10¢,* and *Quarter 25¢.*

2. Provide each child with a 9" x 12" sheet of construction paper and an equal number of pennies, nickels, dimes, and quarters. Show the children how to fold their construction paper to form four sections similar to those on the overhead projector. Ask them to label each section as shown.

3. Display a penny and have children find a coin like it in their collections. Ask them to identify the coin and say its value.

4. As you model with your overhead collection, ask the children to locate all the pennies in their collections and place them in the appropriate section of their construction paper workmats.

5. Repeat the procedure with the nickels, dimes, and quarters.

6. Ask the class to help you find the value of the collections placed in each of their sections. Make sure the children note that pennies are counted by ones since they are worth 1¢, nickels by fives since they are worth 5¢, and so on.

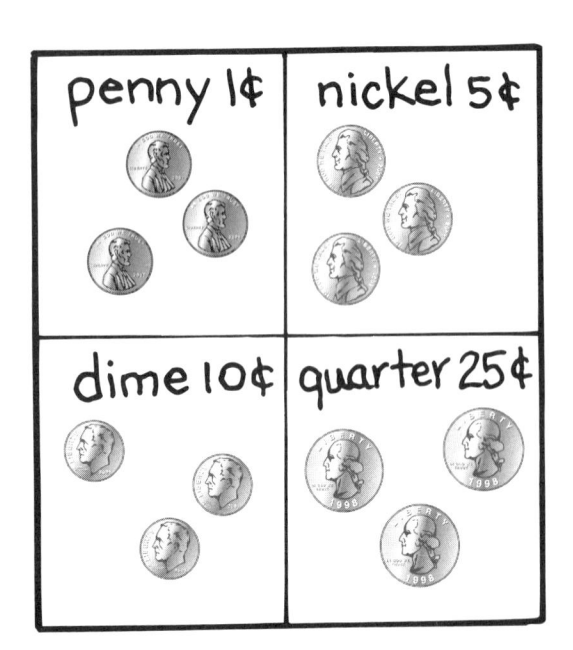

Counting Coin Collections on a Hundred Chart

Transparency 1

This activity offers an alternate approach to counting coin collections.

1. Provide each child with a slightly enlarged copy of the *Hundred Chart* transparency, along with a collection of five pennies, six or more nickels, ten or more dimes, and four quarters.

2. Ask children to name the value of a dime (10¢). Have them place dimes on the 10 square on their charts, then on every tenth place thereafter to 100.

3. Ask the children to remove one of their dimes at a time and to circle the sections beneath them.

4. Ask the children to name the value of a nickel (5¢). Have children place nickels on the 5 square on their charts, then on every fifth place thereafter to 50.

5. Ask the children to remove one of their nickels at a time and to color the sections yellow beneath them.

6. Encourage children to note that every second yellow section is also circled; therefore two nickels have the same value as a dime.

7. Remind children that quarters are worth 25¢. Have children place red dots in the corners of the squares with numbers 25, 50, 75, and 100.

8. Once the squares are marked, have the children use the charts to count coin collections as follows:

    a. Have the children place in their hands three dimes, one nickel, and four pennies.

    b. Have the children place the three dimes on the 10, 20, and 30 squares.

    c. Have the children place the nickel on the next yellow square on their charts: 35.

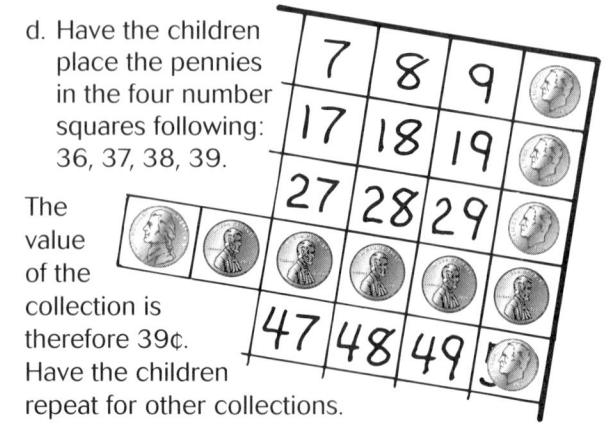

    d. Have the children place the pennies in the four number squares following: 36, 37, 38, 39.

The value of the collection is therefore 39¢. Have the children repeat for other collections.

© Judy/Instructo

J331001 Clearly Math • Grade 1

Name _____ Time to the Hour

Hour Match Game

Match.

A.		6 o'clock	3:00
B.		3 o'clock	6:00
C.		12 o'clock	8:00
D.		9 o'clock	12:00
E.		8 o'clock	4:00
F.		4 o'clock	9:00

© Judy/Instructo

Name _____ Telling Time to the Half Hour

The Wrong Time

Which one is wrong? Cross it out.

A.

3:00   half past 3

B.

10:30   10 o'clock

C.

2:30   2 o'clock

D.

1:00   half past 1

E.

7:00   half past 7

F.

11:30   11 o'clock

Name _____   Showing Time on a Clock

The Hands of Time

Here is Sam's schedule.

8:00	Wake up.
9:30	Start school.
4:30	Play soccer.
6:00	Eat dinner.
8:00	Read a book.
8:30	Go to bed.

Draw the hands on each clock to match the time.

A. 8:00
Wake up.

B. 9:30
Start school.

C. 4:30
Play soccer.

D. 6:00
Eat dinner.

E. 8:00
Read a book.

F. 8:30
Go to bed.

G. What time do you go to bed? _____

© Judy/Instructo

41
Reproducible

J331001 Clearly Math • Grade 1

Name _____   Measuring in Inches

Inch by Inch

Measure the lines with your ruler. Circle the correct number.

Write the letters at the bottom to find the secret word.

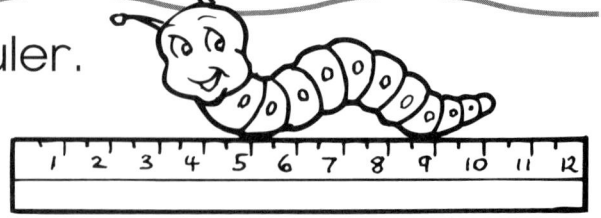

A. |——————|
    1 inch   2 inches   3 inches

E. |————————————————|
    2 inches   3 inches   4 inches

S. |——————————————————————————————|
    5 inches   6 inches   7 inches

U. |————————————————————|
    5 inches   4 inches   3 inches

R. |————————————————————————————————|
    6 inches   5 inches   4 inches

M. |————————|
    4 inches   3 inches   2 inches

___ ___ ___ ___ ___ ___ ___
 2   3   1   5   4   6   3

Name _____ Choosing Coins to Pay for Items **T4**

Shopping for Stickers

Tell how much the stickers will cost in all.
Circle the coins whose values will add up to the cost.

A.

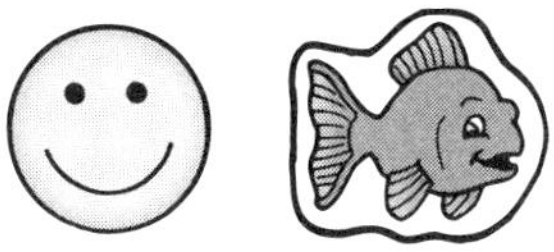

Total cost: _____ ¢

B.

Total cost: _____ ¢

C.

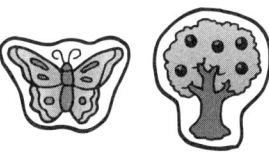

Total cost: _____ ¢

D.

Total cost: _____ ¢

E.

Total cost: _____ ¢

F.

Total cost: _____ ¢

© Judy/Instructo

43
Reproducible

J331001 Clearly Math • Grade 1

Name _____   Counting Coin Collections

Mystery Purse

Write how much.

I. (quarter, penny, penny, penny) ____¢

S. (dime, dime, dime, dime, penny, penny) ____¢

O. (quarter, nickel) ____¢

N. (quarter, quarter, penny) ____¢

C. (dime, dime, dime, dime, nickel) ____¢

Write the letter that matches each amount.

___ ___ ___ ___ ___
45¢ 30¢ 28¢ 51¢ 42¢

What is in the mystery purse? _____

© Judy/Instructo   44   J331001 Clearly Math • Grade 1
                            Reproducible

Name _____ Using Different Coins to Show the Same Amount

Pocket Change

Circle the correct coins.

penny   nickel   dime   quarter

A. Show 15¢ with 3 coins.

B. Show 15¢ with 2 coins.

C. Show 36¢ with 5 coins.

D. Show 36¢ with 3 coins.

E. Show 50¢ with 5 coins.

F. Show 50¢ with 2 coins.

G. You have 2 coins worth a total of 10¢.
What are they? Draw them.

© Judy/Instructo

45
Reproducible

J331001 Clearly Math • Grade 1

DATA AND PROBABILITY

Sorting Rules

Transparency 4

In this activity, children are invited to be creative about how they could sort a group of stickers. Challenge the children to find several ways to sort.

1. Display the *Sticker Store* transparency.

2. Say, "Suppose you want to put these stickers on two different pages of your sticker book. How could you sort them for each page? What sorting rules could you use?"

3. Allow children a few moments to think; then have them share their ideas with the class.

4. After children have had time to share, ask a volunteer to describe the rule he or she devised to sort the stickers. Write the student's classification headings on the chalkboard. Ask his or her classmates to identify stickers that would be classified under each heading.

5. Invite other children to suggest different sorting rules. Continue until several sorting rules have been explored. Help the children see that objects can be sorted in a variety of ways.

Favorite Color Bar Graph

Transparency 8

This activity encourages children to learn something about each other and themselves and enables you to find out what they know about making and interpreting bar graphs.

1. Select a five-color assortment of connecting cubes. You may wish to use red, green, yellow, blue, and black. Record the color names on the *Graphing Grid* transparency along the vertical axis of the bar graph.

2. Reproduce the *Graphing Grid* transparency, including the color names, and distribute a copy to each child. Tell the children that they will make bar graphs that show which colors members of the class prefer.

3. Invite one child at a time up to the overhead projector. Each child should hold up the cube showing his or her favorite color among those provided, say the color's name, then place it on the appropriate color row of the bar graph. You may wish to write the color names on the transparency. Continue until all children have had turns placing cubes on the bar graph or until one color row runs out of space. Have the children write the results on their own sheets.

4. Ask the children to write titles for their bar graphs. Remind them that the titles should describe what the graph shows.

5. Have children write paragraphs describing what they could find out by reading the bar graphs. Encourage them to write everything they can think of, including which color was most popular, which color was least popular, how many people chose the same color they did, and so on.

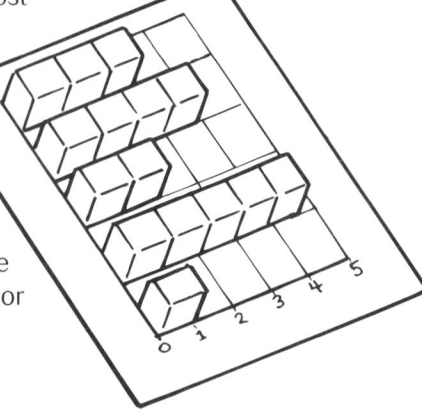

Exploring Probability

1. Ask the children to respond to the following statements with *yes, maybe,* or *no:*

    a. It will rain tomorrow. (Maybe.)

    b. My dog can talk. (No.)

    c. I will get mail today. (Maybe.)

    d. The sun will set tonight. (Yes.)

    e. We will drink something today. (Yes.)

    f. A fish can learn to fly. (No.)

    g. A flower can go for a walk. (No.)

    h. A cat weighs less than a dog. (Maybe.)

2. Invite the children to make up their own probability statements. When you have checked children's statements and answers for accuracy, allow them time to challenge their classmates to solve them.

Coin Pictograph

Transparencies 7 & 8

This partner activity reinforces coin sorting and graphing skills.

1. Reproduce and distribute the *Graphing Grid* transparency.

2. Supply each child in each pair with a random collection of coins. Have the children sort them by type.

3. Show the children how to label the graph by sketching each coin to the left of a row.

4. Ask the children to place coins on their graphing grids to create the pictograph. Model the procedure on the overhead with the coins from the *Rulers and Coins* transparency and the *Graphing Grid* transparency. Have the children check to make sure that their partners' coins are sorted correctly on the graph.

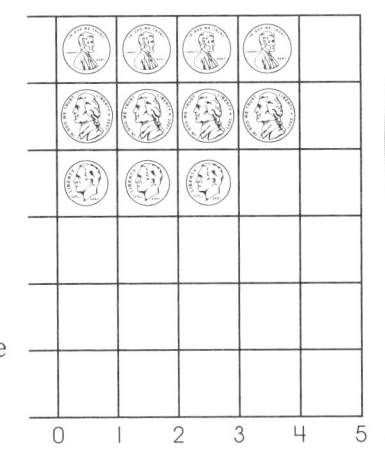

5. Have partners ask each other two questions about their graphs. Questions may include: "Which coin do you have the most?" "How many nickels do you have?" "What is the total value of the dimes on your graph?"

Two-Color Patterns

Transparency 3

1. Cut out the two-color counters from the *Ten-Frames and Two-Color Counters* transparency and display them on the overhead projector.

2. Line up a six-item alternating pattern starting with a red counter on the overhead. Cover the sixth counter.

3. Ask children to say the counter colors aloud ("red, yellow, red, yellow, red").

4. Ask a volunteer to predict the color that will come next in the pattern (yellow).

5. Ask the children to describe the pattern and to tell how they could use it to make predictions. (The pattern "takes turns" for red and yellow; and it's yellow's turn.)

6. Remove the counters and create another pattern. Repeat the process.

7. Ask a volunteer to make up a pattern for his or her classmates to extend. Encourage the children to explain or justify alternative ideas for extending some patterns.

8. Once the children are familiar with creating and extending patterns, allow them to explore more patterns with two-color counters or reproduced and colored counters.

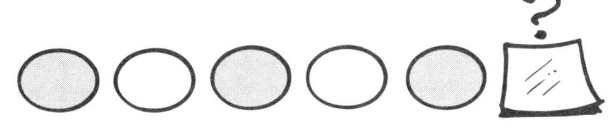

Name _____ Making Tally Tables

Playtime Table

Make a tally table.
Show all you see.

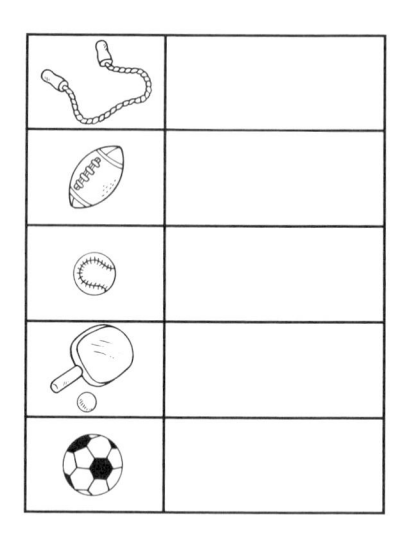

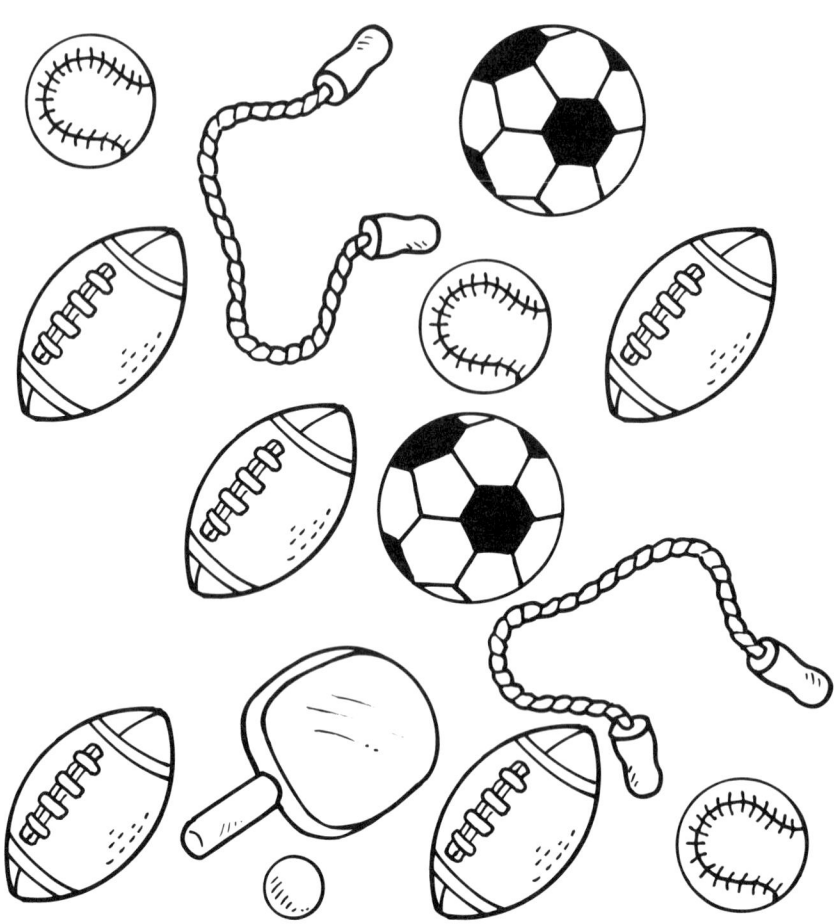

Use your tally table.

A. How many?

🪢 ____ ⚾ ____ 🏈 ____ ⚽ ____ 🏓 ____

B. Which had the most? 🏈 ⚾ 🪢

C. Which had the fewest? 🏈 ⚾ 🏓

D. Which two had the same amount? 🏈 ⚽ 🪢

48
Reproducible

© Judy/Instructo   J331001 Clearly Math • Grade 1

Name _____   Reading a Pictograph

Picture This!

People picked their favorite foods.
Read the pictograph.
Answer the questions.

Our Favorite Foods

	1	2	3	4	5	6
cookie	🍪	🍪	🍪	🍪	🍪	🍪
ice cream	🍦	🍦	🍦	🍦	🍦	
pretzel	🥨	🥨	🥨	🥨		
candy	🍬	🍬	🍬			
apple	🍎	🍎	🍎	🍎	🍎	

A. Which food was picked the most? _____

B. Which food was picked the least? _____

C. Which two foods were picked just as often?

_____ and _____

D. How many people picked foods in all? _____

E. How many more people picked 🥨 than 🍬? ____

Name _____   Making a Bar Graph T5

Pattern Block Graph

Complete the bar graph.

Pattern Blocks

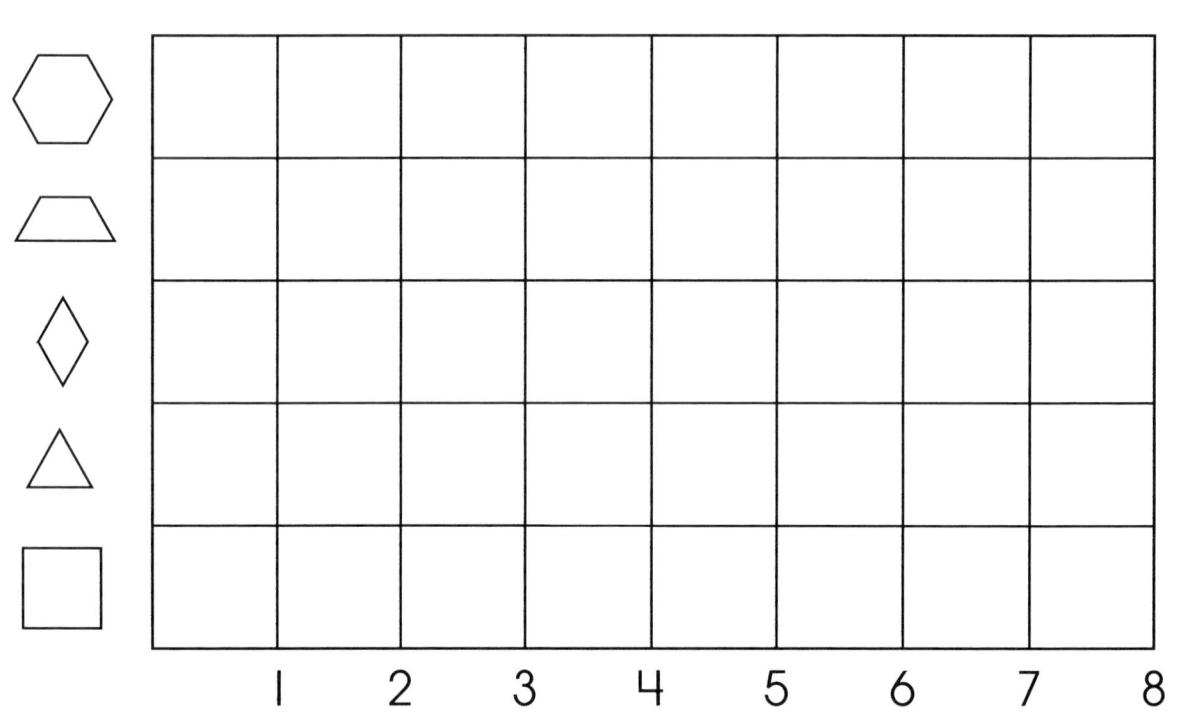

Answer the questions.

A. How many?

⬡ ____   ⬠ ____   ◇ ____   △ ____   □ ____

B. How many more △ than □ ? ____

C. How many fewer ◇ than ⬡ ? ____

D. How many pattern blocks in all? ____

Pattern Power

Which comes next? Circle it.

A.

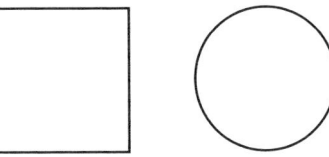

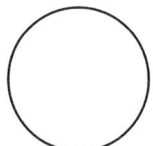

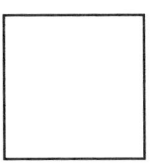

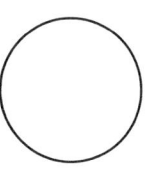

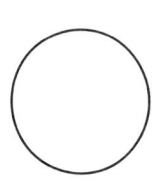

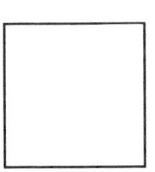

B.

C.

D. 1 3 3 3 1 3 3 3 | 1 3

E. ↑ → ↓ ↑ → ↓ ↑ → | ↓ ↑

F. Make up your own pattern.

Name _____

Dot Paper

Teacher: Use this page with "Same Size and Shape" (page 30).

Name _____

Pattern Blocks

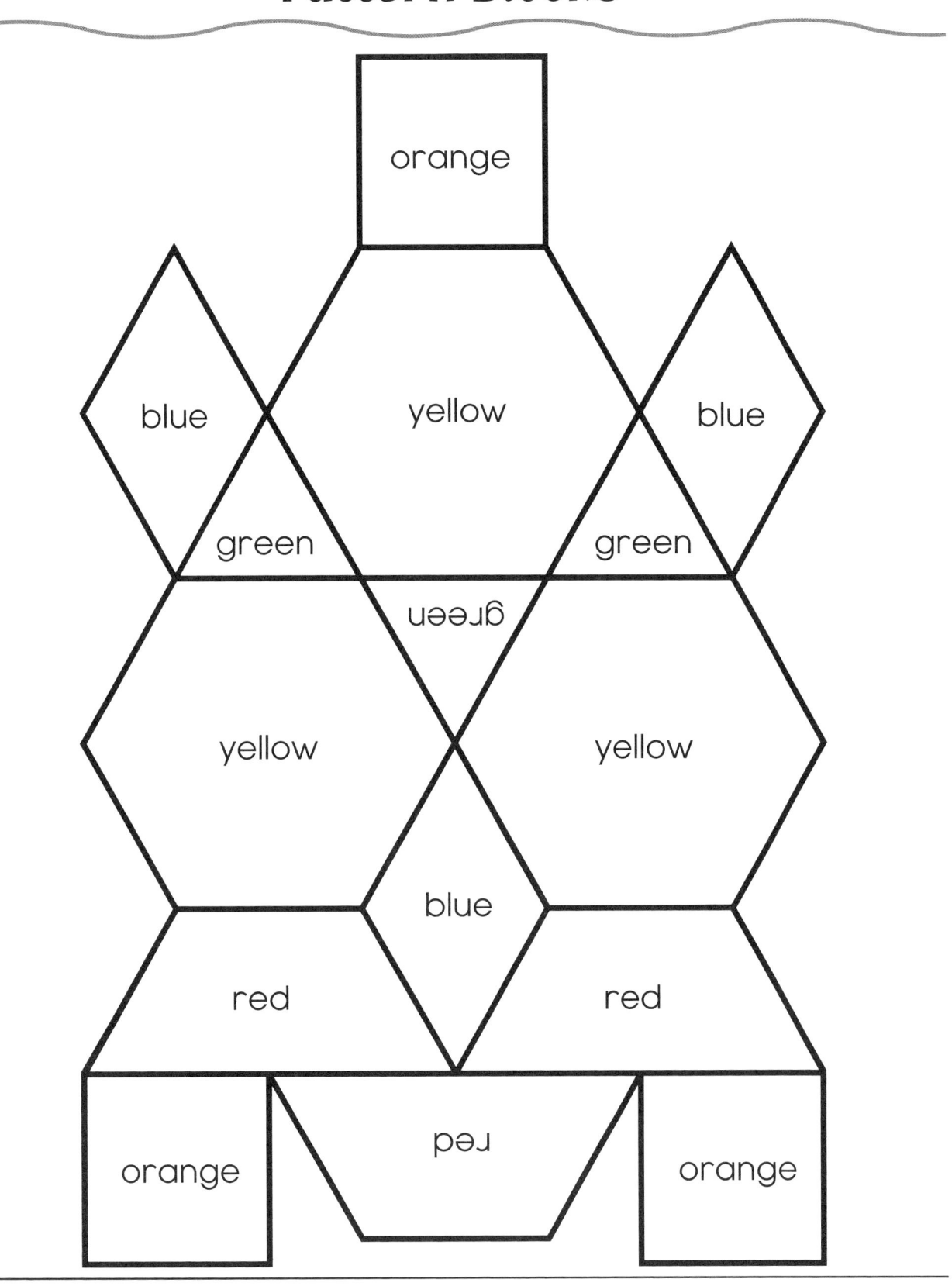

orange

blue   yellow   blue

green   green

green

yellow   yellow

blue

red   red

orange   red   orange

Teacher: See page 31 for directions on how to use this page.

© Judy/Instructo   Reproducible   J331001 Clearly Math • Grade 1

Answers

Page 7
Responses will vary. Dots should match numerals.

Page 8
Match.

	tens	ones	
A.	3	7	75
B.	7	5	43
C.	4	3	52
D.	5	2	37
E.	8	1	18
F.	1	8	59
G.	5	9	81

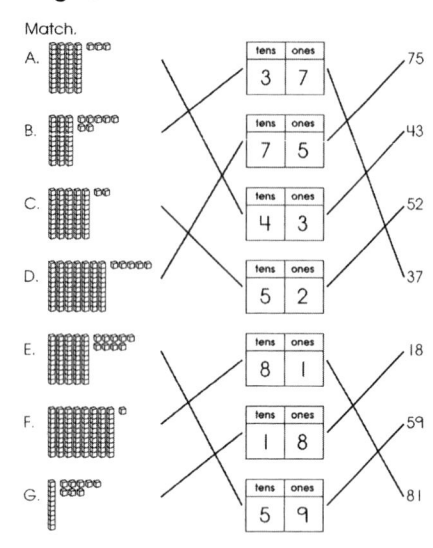

Page 9

10 < 9	26 < 30	19 > 91
90 > 78	44 < 34	17 < 81
26 > 29	15 < 19	20 < 19
30 > 32	92 < 95	81 > 89
83 < 75	27 > 24	62 < 49
58 < 60	19 > 20	29 > 21
56 > 85	18 > 16	79 > 81

Page 10
The shape is a sun.

Page 11
A. **24**, 47   B. 37, 16
C. 31, 88   D. 82, 69
E. 45, 94   F. +1
G. −1   H. +10
I. −10

Page 14
(butterfly coloring)

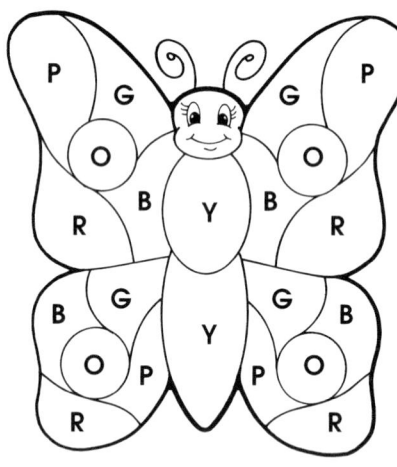

Page 15
1. 14, 12, 11   2. 15, 13, 18
3. 17, 16, 13   4. 11, 10, 15
TEN IS SPECIAL

Page 16
A. 6 + 6 = 12   B. 8 + 8 = 16
C. 7 + 7 = 14   D. 9 + 9 = 18
E. 6 + 6 = 12, so 6 + 7 = 13.
F. 7 + 7 = 14, so 7 + 8 = 15.
G. 8 + 8 = 16, so 8 + 9 = 17.
H. 9 + 9 = 18, so 9 + 10 = 19.

Page 17
8 + 4 = 12   10 + 1 = 11
6 + 9 = 15   10 + 2 = 12
7 + 6 = 13   10 + 5 = 15
2 + 9 = 11   10 + 3 = 13
5 + 9 = 14   10 + 8 = 18
8 + 8 = 16   10 + 7 = 17
8 + 9 = 17   10 + 4 = 14
9 + 9 = 18   10 + 6 = 16

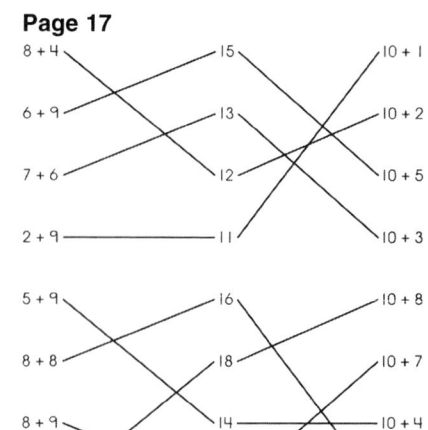

Page 18
A. **3¢ + 8¢ = 11¢**   B. 4¢ + 5¢ = 9¢
C. 9¢ + 6¢ = 15¢   D. 7¢ + 8¢ = 15¢
E. 2¢ + 4¢ = 6¢   F. 5¢ + 7¢ = 12¢
G. 7¢ + 6¢ = 13¢   H. 9¢ + 8¢ = 17¢
I. Answers will vary.

Page 19
A. 22, 29, 90, 18, 42
B. 50, 55, 81, 32, 58
C. 82, 69, 60, 37, 95
D. 52, 56, 70, 94, 80

B	I	N	G	O
22	56	20	82	18
32	29	12	70	69
14	58	60	90	94
50	13	37	80	81
52	95	42	55	10

Page 23
(house coloring: yellow, orange, blue, purple, red, green)

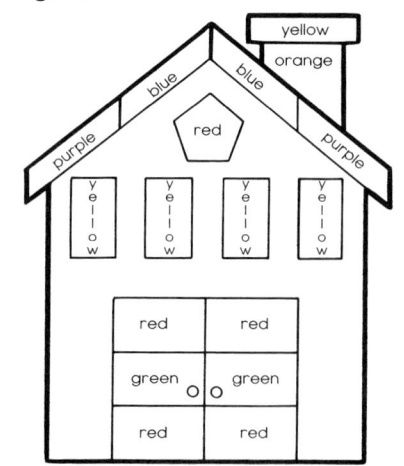

Page 24

A.
16	7	9
8	1	7
8	6	2

B.
13	5	8
4	0	4
9	5	4

C.
18	9	9
10	2	8
8	7	1

D.
15	6	9
9	3	6
6	3	3

E.
17	9	8
8	7	1
9	2	7

F. Answers will vary.

Page 25
A. 5 in the bag B. 2 in the bag
C. 5 in the bag D. 5 in the bag
E. 6 in the bag F. 0 in the bag
G. 4 in the bag H. 2 in the bag
I. Possible answer: Count on from the counters to the totals.

Page 26
A. 5¢ − 3¢ = 2¢   B. 4¢ − 2¢ = 2¢
C. 9¢ − 5¢ = 4¢   D. 7¢ − 2¢ = 5¢
E. 6¢ − 4¢ = 2¢   F. 8¢ − 3¢ = 5¢
G. The auto sticker is 2¢ less.
H. The smiley face sticker is 5¢ less.

Page 27
A. 6 + 4 = 10, 4 + 6 = 10
   10 − 6 = 4, 10 − 4 = 6
B. 7 + 5 = 12, 5 + 7 = 12
   12 − 7 = 5, 12 − 5 = 7
C. 5 + 8 = 13, 8 + 5 = 13
   13 − 8 = 5, 13 − 5 = 8
D. 9 + 6 = 15, 6 + 9 = 15
   15 − 9 = 6, 15 − 6 = 9

Page 28

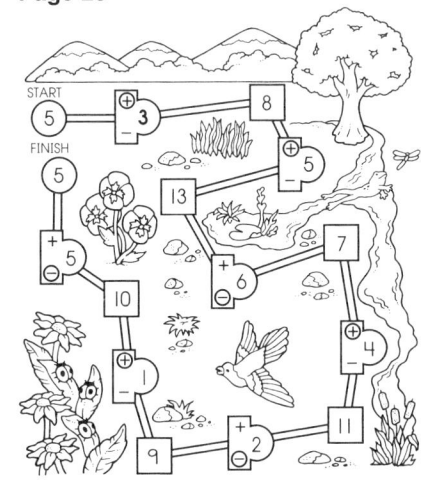

Page 29
Across
A. 53 − 3 = 50   B. 80 − 3 = 77
C. 21 − 8 = 13   E. 44 − 5 = 39
F. 70 − 7 = 63   G. 20 − 7 = 13
H. 65 − 5 = 60   I. 29 − 4 = 25
J. 13 − 5 = 8   K. 46 + 4 = 50
Down
A. 58 − 1 = 57   B. 79 − 6 = 73
C. 22 − 3 = 19   D. 21 − 8 = 13
E. 38 − 5 = 33   F. 68 − 8 = 60
G. 11 − 1 = 10   H. 71 − 6 = 65
I. 29 − 9 = 20   J. 90 − 8 = 82

Page 32
1. S (cylinder)   2. H (sphere)
3. A (cone)   4. P (rect. solid)
5. E (cone)
The secret word is SHAPE.

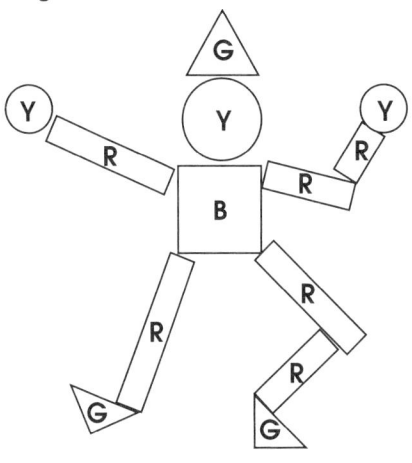

Page 33
Six rectangles; three triangles; one square; three circles

Page 34

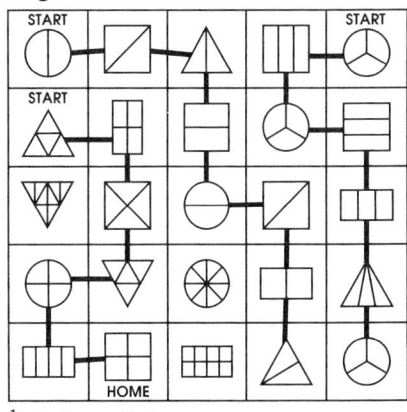

Page 35
¼ is the path home.

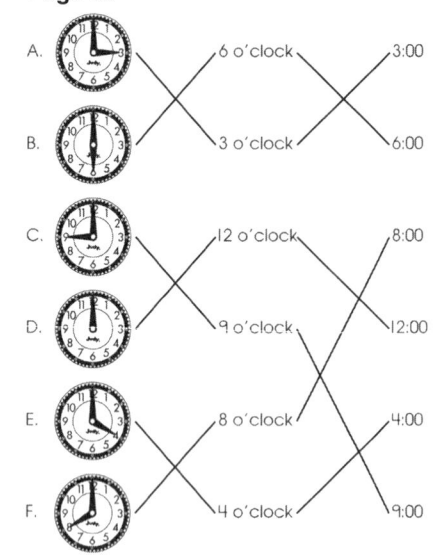

Page 39
A. 6 o'clock — 3:00
B. 3 o'clock — 6:00
C. 12 o'clock — 8:00
D. 9 o'clock — 12:00
E. 8 o'clock — 4:00
F. 4 o'clock — 9:00

Page 40
A. ~~3:00~~ half past 3
B. 10:30 ~~10 o'clock~~
C. 2:30 ~~2 o'clock~~
D. ~~1:00~~ half past 1
E. ~~7:00~~ half past 7
F. 11:30 ~~11 o'clock~~

Page 41
G. Answers will vary.

Page 42
A. 1 inch   E. 3 inches
S. 5 inches U. 4 inches
R. 6 inches M. 2 inches
MEASURE

Page 43
Note: circled coins may vary.
A. Total cost: 8¢
B. Total cost: 13¢
C. Total cost: 6¢
D. Total cost: 10¢
E. Total cost: 12¢
F. Total cost: 15¢

Page 44
I. 28¢   S. 42¢
O. 30¢   N. 51¢
C. 45¢
What is in the mystery purse? COINS.

Page 45
A. 3 nickels
B. 1 dime, 1 nickel
C. 3 dimes, 1 nickel, 1 penny
D. 1 quarter, 1 dime, 1 penny
E. 5 dimes
F. 2 quarters
G. 2 nickels

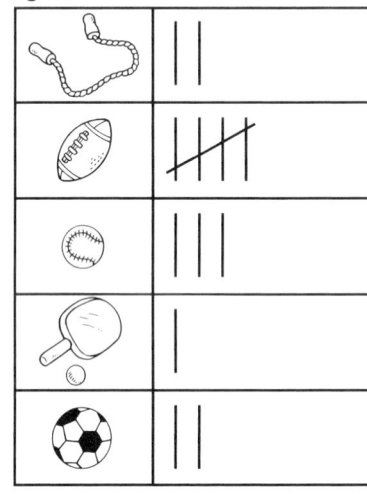

Page 48
A. 2 jump ropes, 3 baseballs, 5 footballs, 2 soccer balls, 1 ball with paddle
B. Which had the most?: football
C. Which had the fewest?: ball with paddle
D. Which two had the same amount?: soccer ball, jump rope

Page 49
A. Cookie
B. Candy
C. Fruit and Ice Cream
D. 23
E. 1

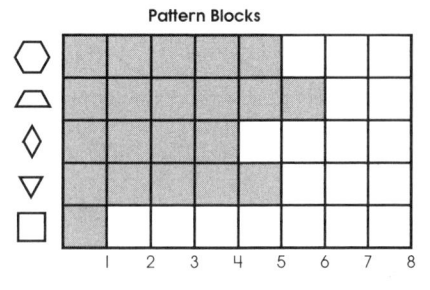

Page 50
A. 5 hexagons, 6 trapezoids, 4 rhombi, 5 triangles, 1 square
B. 4 more triangles than squares
C. 1 fewer rhombi than hexagons
D. 21 pattern blocks in all

Page 51
A. (square, circle, square, circle, circle, square — last circled)
B. (coins — last circled)
C. (triangle, circle, triangle, circle, triangle, triangle — last circled)
D. 1 3 3 3 1 3 3 3 ⓘ 3
E. ↑ → ↓ ↑ → ↓ ↑ → ⓓ ↑
F. Patterns will vary.